Table of Contents

Introduction

For several years, Youth Communication made a special effort to bring teenage girls together to discuss and write about the important issues, experiences, and relationships in their lives.

Our "Girls Writing Groups" were inspired in part by our reading of the growing literature documenting the difficulties adolescent girls have developing and maintaining a strong sense of self. In public, girls often find it hard to just be themselves. There's so much pressure to be attractive, sexy, popular, feminine, and grown up. In their writing, on the other hand, girls find it much easier to explore who they really are. They can express their true feelings, voice their confusion about what's expected of them, and grapple with who they really want to be.

In the stories collected here, the writers describe their thoughts and feelings with openness and honesty. These young women describe their struggles to become comfortable with themselves, even if they're not meeting their parents' expectations or fitting in with their friends. Their writing will provide readers (particularly other teenage girls) with a model for reflecting on and clarifying their own confusions and conflicts, a process that can help them feel more in control of their own lives.

The first section, "Growing Up Girl" contains stories about moving from girlhood to womanhood. The authors raise the question, "What does it mean to be a woman?" and struggle to come up with definitions of femininity and ways to express their developing sexuality that feel comfortable, not forced. This process involves sorting out the mixed—and conflicting—messages they get from parents, peers, and the media about how they are supposed to look and behave.

The stories show how difficult it is for young women to develop at their own pace—emotionally and physically. In the first two stories, both authors describe wondering, "What's wrong with me?" when it seemed like all the other girls their age suddenly had breasts and boyfriends and sexy clothes while they still looked and felt like little girls. These stories will help young women who feel different and out-of-sync understand that, in fact, everyone is different and that figuring out who you are and who you want to be is a process that takes time, reflection, and experimentation.

These stories are also about the authors' journeys from passive acceptance of their parents' values to active questioning and rebellion against them.

In the second section, "Family Matters," our writers address in greater detail the messages they get from their parents about what's expected of them as girls and how they feel about and deal with those expectations.

As these stories show, for many young women, particularly those from immigrant families, the ideals of female behavior they get at home are often in conflict with what they hear from the media and the larger society. Outside the home, they may be hearing that men and women are equal and that girls can aspire to be anything they choose, but at home they may find themselves given more responsibility, but less freedom, than their brothers. In the media, they may see images of women postponing marriage and children but still having active sex lives, while at home they may be deemed "sluts" for expressing any interest in boys.

These conflicting messages are highlighted in the four pieces entitled, "Mama Said." Inspired by the short story "Girl" by Jamaica Kincaid, in which a mother lectures her daughter about appropriate womanly behavior, these young women write in the voices of their mothers, laying out the advice, rules, and suggestions they are bombarded with at home. The popular notion that young men and women receive equal treatment nowadays is undercut by such motherly comments as, "Girls play like girls and boys play like boys," "Sit like a lady," "Why do you have to keep asking why your brother doesn't have to do this and you do—is it that you want to be a man now?" "You're gonna have to cook...because...you know how men like to eat."

The other stories in this section explore how young women feel about the rules, expectations, and double standards that define their relationships with their families, as well as how they cope with them.

The stories in Section 3, "How Do We Look?" explore the relationship between appearances and identity. The way young women look and dress, a frequent source of tension between girls and their families, can also play an important role in the development of peer relationships. Clothing styles can express personality, tastes in music, and favorite pastimes and can help like-minded teens find each other. For adolescent girls in particular, clothes can express their acceptance or rejection of cultural standards of femininity and sexual attractiveness. How they dress may be a way of saying, "Look at me! I'm a woman now!" or "Leave me alone, I'm just a little girl."

But while girls can experiment with the way they dress, they have much less control over their physical appearance. Part of growing up is coming to terms with how you look and accepting yourself for who you are. In "Big, Black, and Beautiful" the author has to battle both racial and gender stereotypes about how she should look and act. It's not until she moves to a new school, where teens are more diverse and accepting, that she starts to feel good about the way she looks and focus on other parts of her life, like improving her grades.

The stories in Section 4, "Together/Apart" look at sexuality and romantic relationships. The writers are gay and straight. Some are sexually active and others are not. All of them are trying to figure out what they want, what's right for them, how to balance their desires against the need to protect themselves from physical and/or emotional harm, and how to achieve relationships based on mutual trust and respect.

Street harassment is a common problem for adolescent girls. While girls are sometimes flattered by the attention, more often it makes them feel self-conscious, embarrassed, afraid, confused, disgusted, and angry. In Section 5, "Hey Baby: You Look Good," three young women describe their experiences with this kind of sexual harassment, sort through their feelings, and try to figure out how to respond. Are they inviting unwanted attention with the way they dress? Should they try to teach guys a lesson by giving them a taste of their own medicine? What's it like for a girl to openly admire a guy's body? Where do we draw the line between flirting and sexual harassment?

We hope young women reading these stories will find comfort, support, useful information, new insights, and even a few laughs. We hope reading it will make them feel less alone and maybe even inspire them to do some writing about their own lives. But this book isn't just for girls. We hope their parents, teachers, brothers, and boyfriends will read it too—in order to get a better understanding of what the young women in their lives are going through and some help in raising sensitive issues that can be hard to talk about.

In the following stories, some names have been changed: *"Ready for Mr. Right,"* and *"A Very Fine #9 Cutie."*

Part 1: Growing Up Girl

YC Art Dept.

Womanhood Can Wait

By Nicole Hawkins

Sometimes, when I'm walking down the block, I'll see a 12-year-old girl with hardly any clothes on and I'll wonder if this little girl knows something more than I know. What inside of her makes her want to possess and execute such sexuality when it is too much for me to deal with? She seems in a rush to capture something that seems so much bigger than the two of us: womanhood.

I am 18 years old, but I'm not exactly sure if I'm an 18-year-old woman or an 18-year-old girl. Lots of times I feel like I'm on my way. But other times I feel clueless, like everything is still new and a mystery to me. It seems like girls are always in a hurry to grow up and become women—and part of being a woman means having boyfriends and having sex. But I'm still struggling to understand who I am, and I'm not sure I'm ready for womanhood yet.

When I was little I loved to play Barbies. Barbie was her own woman. She was beautiful, intelligent, and powerful. My Barbie was a teacher by day and a babe by night. She was sexy, feminine, and proud. Through Barbie and Ken, I would act out making love and how it related to the perfect relationship.

When they had sex, Barbie usually was a virgin and Ken wasn't. She wouldn't regret it, though, because it was the final big act of true love. Later she would feel nervous that her father would find out and disown her, but when he did find out, he realized that she was happy, and just loved and supported her. That was love and sex in my fantasy world. In reality, things were more complicated.

At a young age I was taught that boys were bad while girls were nice and made up of sugar and spice. I was told to defend myself against boys any way I knew how, including scratching their eyeballs out. One day when I was 6 years old, I was sitting on the couch with my legs spread wide apart. For no apparent reason my father slapped them shut. Little did I know this was my first lesson on sex. Lesson #1: It's bad to sit with your legs open.

I watched my sister become involved with boys and get hurt, either dumped or cheated on, and it made me glad that my turn was ages away.

I was told that if I had sex before I got married, I would be disowned and put in a home. Maybe my father felt that since he waited until he was about 22 years old to have sex with my mother, I, a female, should have no problem holding out. My mother was even worse. If I had sex before marriage, I would not only be considered a disappointment, but worst of all, a SLUT!

Despite these lectures, I was still very close to my father. Besides instilling in me fear, my father built up my self-esteem and taught me to do things for myself. He would say things like, "You have to do well in school so that you can be accepted into a good college, so you can be your own woman and won't have to depend on a man," and I believed him. He taught me to depend on myself. At the same time, he made me feel like it was OK to be a kid.

Even after I started dating, my father still bought me Barbie doll stuff to add to my collection. I remember feeling happy, relieved, and confused all at the same time. While I was facing the idea that sooner or later I had to grow up, here was my daddy telling me, "It's OK to be a kid for as long as you can."

When I was 8 years old, my 11-year-old sister, Tamika, started puberty. It seemed like such a dreadful thing. Yuck, the acne, PMS, cramps, awkwardness, boobs, and boys. It just reinforced all the things my father had told me. Growing up was not fun. It was supposed to mean taking responsibility for yourself and your actions. Instead I watched my sister's body and emotions control her, and then I watched her get grounded for acting irresponsibly.

Unlike with Barbie and Ken, where love was safe and predictable, in the real-life situations my sister was in, everything seemed like a tailspin. I watched my sister become involved with boys and get hurt, either dumped or cheated on, and it made me glad that my turn was ages away. What a joy, I thought, to be able to lie on my stomach and be comfortable because my chest was completely flat. Part of me wanted to remain a little girl always.

Still, all around me people were maturing. By junior high school, the rest of my peers seemed to be well into their third or fourth relationship. I felt like something was wrong with me, unnatural. I felt like it was my duty to act mature, so I went a little boy crazy myself.

I had already had my first kiss when my mother decided to explore the pages of my diary. She called me a slut and a harlot and threatened to put me in a home. I was terrified by her reaction but a part of me wanted to show her what rebellion really was. Then something happened that stopped me dead in my tracks.

My friend Sharnette and I used to hang out and get ourselves into these fine little messes. When we were 13, Sharnette started dating this guy Ricky. Ricky had a friend, Edgar, who wanted to get hooked up with me. Edgar was cute and four years older than me. So Sharnette and I visited the boys at Ricky's house. Edgar and I sat on the bed and talked and played video games. Then we started to kiss.

Soon Edgar began to massage my breasts. Immediately I wanted to put an end to the situation, but before I could act he was pulling the ends of my shirt out of my pants. I began to panic. I had no idea where the situation was going. I stood up in a rush and proclaimed that I was leaving. A couple of months later I found out that Edgar was planning to have sex with me that evening.

After that, I became fearful of guys and all my parents' warnings raced through my head. Foolishly, I'd believed I was mature enough to handle a situation that was way over my head. I started to see guys as the unpredictable, conniving creatures my father described. I still wanted to explore my sexuality, but I didn't feel safe anymore.

By the time high school started, I was also feeling more self-conscious about my body. The summer before high school, I grew a few inches and my chest swelled up to a C cup. While lots of teenage girls like attention from the opposite sex, I didn't. I hated when guys would stare at my chest and look to see if I had a nice ass. I wore baggy jeans and plaid shirts big enough to hide the protruding obstacles settled in my bra. I became extremely shy around everyone, especially boys.

For the first couple of years of high school, I don't think I even said a full sentence. Even though I was having a really hard time, I also grew a lot. Being alone so much gave me space and time to explore who I was and would ultimately become. I started to become my own leader, dancing to the beat of my drum.

When I was around 14 and 15, I began to question my father's beliefs. I'd tell my father that I didn't know if I could wait until I got married to have sex. He thought I was in a rebellious, disrespectful stage. He was partially right, but not fully. I also really wanted answers about sex. I didn't want to be told that I was too young to understand, so I turned to other sources. I started reading a lot of magazines, like *Mademoiselle* and *Vogue*. They were full of images of new "Barbies" for me to marvel at. On the radio I discovered a show called "Love Phones" with Dr. Judy Kurianski. I would tune in every Monday through Thursday and listen to her talk about topics such as homosexuality, AIDS, cheating, virginity, femininity, even different sexual positions.

Over the next couple of years, I began to gain control of my life. My schoolwork improved, and I became very spiritual for a while. I felt like I was rediscovering myself. I also began to feel that the sexuality that was sprouting in me was natural and shouldn't be looked upon as evil. Last fall, I entered an alternative school and soared academically. I even joined the school newspaper. I was really confident and proud of myself. I also had a job.

By finding stability in other areas of my life, I was able to begin to feel comfortable about my body and my sexuality. For the first time in a long time I felt comfortable enough to allow myself to be emotionally vulnerable. I was ready to take on the responsibility of relationships. Soon I developed friendships with males and I no longer felt threatened.

This past year, my senior year of high school, I have really transformed. I have been living with my best friend and her family for a year because there were just too many arguments at home, and my parents agreed it would be better. I have also been working. I'm not completely independent, but for the first time in my life I feel somewhat in control and really liberated.

When I first moved in with my friend, I still wore baggy pants and no makeup. But I noticed that after my 18th birthday, my pants began to get tighter, my shirts began to get smaller, and I began to stare into the mirror, pouting and perfecting lining my lips.

There are times these days when I'll put on a dress and suddenly I'll feel more powerful. Occasionally you'll see me walking down the street, strutting with such self-confidence you wouldn't even recognize me. Sometimes dressing feminine can do that to a person.

The other day I found myself in a store looking at lingerie. That's something I'd never thought I would be doing before the Second Coming of Christ. I am actually considering buying a matching bra and panty set even though the price is too high. A little voice inside my head is telling me, "You'll look so sexy and cute in this outfit, you'll be irresistible." Part of me wants to be in the spotlight showing everyone just how beautiful I can be.

There are times these days when I'll put on a dress and suddenly I'll feel more powerful.

Still, I often question the pros and cons of exhibiting my femininity. It seems like it could make me more powerful, more me. But I also worry if it will make me more passive, and more likely to rely on beauty to get by. And sometimes I'll be sitting on the train and I'll look at the professionally dressed women and I'll wonder, what if they're as confused about themselves and life as I am? What if they're just putting on a show to make their colleagues, families, and friends believe they are Woman?

I used to believe that after your teens, you get it all down pat. But as I approach adulthood, I don't find that to be true at all. My current boyfriend and I started dating a week after this past Valentine's Day. With Jamil it was different from the start. Even before we started dating, we were friends. We would listen to each other and make each other laugh. And after we began going out, it was incredible. For the first time in my life I actually trusted a guy almost 100%. That was something I never thought

I would do.

Even though I love Jamil and I can pretty much see myself someday being with him, I don't want to do something I'm not ready for. I have all the time in the world to experience sex. I figure why not wait a while and experience my virginity. I know that my first time will be very intense and will make me feel vulnerable, but I don't want to feel overwhelmed or too out of control of the situation. I want it to be satisfying.

I'm glad that I've decided to be cautious about the choices I make. I'm glad that I've waited and not rushed into sex, because I haven't found myself yet. I still have a lot to figure out.

Nicole was 18 when she wrote this story.

Trying Femininity on for Size

By Debbie Seraphin

Growing up, I was always around boys. I have two older brothers and we have always been very close. So what they did, I did. What they wore, I wore. I climbed gates and walls, rode bikes, and played every type of sport. I dressed in baggy jeans, T-shirts and sneakers. I had no idea what feminine was. The fellas thought it was cool having me around, so I just enjoyed myself, not realizing how all of this was going to affect me later on in my life.

In elementary school, I thought being a tomboy was cool. I didn't stand out that much because everybody dressed like a tomboy back then. The baggy style and hat-to-the-back look were in. The way of dress was very similar for both girls and boys.

When I was around 9, I noticed that other girls weren't like me. They were playing with dolls and having tea parties, things I was not allowed to do. My parents said that playing those games was like preparing to have a baby and a husband and that I was too young to have those ideas in my head. Since I knew my parents wouldn't allow it, I never let myself get too interested in dolls or dress up or other girls' games. I just wanted to know why other girls liked them so much.

To be honest, I wasn't much interested in sports either. What I did enjoy was reading, dancing, and singing. I could do those things by myself and still have a good time. But since my brothers were always playing sports and my parents made me go everywhere with them, I had no choice.

Still, I was basically happy with who I was until I arrived in junior high school. That was a period of hell. The kids would call me a tomboy because I wore baggy jeans, sweatshirts, and braids in my hair. To make things worse, I was taller and skinnier than all the rest of the girls and I was underdeveloped. The other kids would hit me in my chest and say that they couldn't be hurting me, because I had nothing there. They would say, "Hurry up and grow. Then we won't have to hit you anymore."

One time in art class, a boy came up to me and started dissing on me for the entire period. He said, "Why do you look like you have no chest and no body? All you do is wear those dodo braids in your hair. You are so skinny and ugly. You are never going to change because you are naturally a chickenhead." I cried for the entire period while the rest of the class laughed at me. I was so embarrassed.

I was always asking myself, "Why do I have to look like this, and when am I going to change?"

I believed everything everyone told me to hurt my feelings. I thought I did not deserve to live. I went home crying every day because I did not like myself. I felt like an ugly duckling. In addition to my flat chest, I had skinny legs and knobby knees. I was always asking myself, "Why do I have to look like this, and when am I going to change?"

All of my close friends were already dating. They were pretty and smart and had everything going for them. When they were with their boyfriends, I felt left out. I never told them how I felt because I thought if I opened up, they would just mock me.

When prom night came in the 8th grade, I was determined to prove to myself that I could fit in. This was going to be my big breakthrough. My mom and I went shopping for a new dress and shoes. I wore an elegant purple gown with rhinestones at the straps and black slingback high-heeled pumps. My hair was done in drop curls with a bang in the front. This was the first time I had ever tried to be feminine, my big transformation.

When I first walked in, I was nervous because I didn't know how everyone was going to react to me. But I felt good in my dress and enjoyed the attention I was getting. My friends were surprised at how nice I looked and heads actually turned. Everyone was wondering who the new girl was. I was having a good time. Then, just when I was thinking, "I did it," something had to go wrong.

I was going into the girls' bathroom and a guy walked passed and said, "Shouldn't you be going to the boys' bathroom with me? Because you surely look like a boy to me, Shorty."

Boy, was I pissed! I wanted to curse him out but I didn't have the courage. I went home and cried instead. I had thought this was going to be my night. After all, this was my prom night. But, no! I had to get hurt and be brought down from my one good day in that school.

I decided that when I got to high school, I was going to change. Not just in terms of the way I looked, like I did for the prom. But in terms of how I acted. I wanted to stop being so shy and easily intimidated.

When I went to school on the first day of my freshman year, I decided to study the other girls to get ideas for the new me. I watched the way they talked, dressed, and acted. I saw the older girls always making sure that they were heard, being very sassy with teachers and flirting with the guys in a friendly way. And they were all popular.

I thought there was only one way to be feminine and this was it. I didn't know anything else. So I just picked up on what I saw and copied it, even though it wasn't me. I said to myself, "If I act like they do, I might get the same reaction."

It worked. I became loud, talkative, and rude. I developed a sassy attitude and everyone seemed to like it. I decided to change my appearance too. I processed my hair and started wearing it in various styles that everyone enjoyed. And, day by day, I added something different to my wardrobe.

I started wearing nice small blouses instead of T-shirts, fitted jeans instead of baggy ones, and shoes instead of sneakers. People started to notice that my style was changing for the better. My transformation was going so well that I went a little overboard. My parents had always been very strict with me, especially in terms of how I dressed. No revealing clothing was allowed. But at this point in my life, I wanted attention and all eyes on me.

Now I realize that there are many different ways of acting feminine.

During my junior and senior years, I decided to rebel against my parents. I went from the nice small blouses to short belly tops, from fitted jeans to tight jeans or short skirts, and from shoes to high-heeled hooker boots. My parents went crazy, of course, but dressing like that made me feel positive about myself.

I rebelled in other ways too. My parents were so busy trying to protect me from bad influences that they had never let me sleep over at other people's houses, or go hang out with my friends, or even go to the movies. I was such a goodie two shoes all my life; now it was time for me to spread my wings. I started to stay out late, travel around the city, and go over to my friends' houses.

My parents yelled at me, talked to my teachers, called my friends, invaded my privacy and spied on me. It didn't work, because I was still sneaky in my own small ways. Then they gave up, deciding that I had to learn my own lesson.

At first, I was having such a good time that I didn't pay my parents any mind. Then, during my senior year, I saw the pain I was putting them through and stopped all the running around. I decided to balance my wild side with my old, calmer side.

Now I go out once in a while, but mostly I am busy getting through my first year of college, being an active member of my church, job-hunting, and writing in my spare time. It's taken a long time, but I am finally happy with myself and my self-esteem is over the roof. I no longer worry about fitting in and being liked. I talk to all types of people and go to all types of places and feel accepted and respected. I love to wake up every morning and look at myself in the mirror, because I feel beautiful inside and out. I'm finally being myself and being feminine at the same time.

I never got to be myself until now. My identity always came from everybody else. When I was younger, I was a tomboy because that's what my family wanted me to be. In junior high, I wanted to be seen as feminine, like the other girls, but I didn't know how to change. In high school, I thought there was only one way to be feminine—the rude, sarcastic, flirtatious style the other girls had. I copied their style and I finally fit in, but it still wasn't me.

Now I realize that there are many different ways of acting feminine. There's the classy, sassy, sarcastic way, and there's the polite, respectful, calm-hearted way. Another way is a mixture of both. That's my way. Who I am now and what I look like now make everything I had to go through to get here worth it. So I thank all those fellas who put me through all that persecution in junior high. All of you have made me a better person.

To anyone who is now going through what I went through back then, I say: "It's going to be OK. You will survive." And to the guys who used to hit me in the chest and make fun of me for being undeveloped, I just want you to know: "You cannot hit me anymore, because if you did, you would get the biggest beatdown of your life."

Debbie was 17 when she wrote this story. She attended Bronx Community College and cosmetology school.

Rudá Tillett

Thinking for Myself

By Anonymous

One day, on one of those ridiculous shopping trips that many girls find themselves embarking on for the first time around age 13, I had an encounter that stuck with me. I was walking along Canal Street in New York City with two acquaintances when it started to drizzle. Suddenly, one of the girls, Sarah, dove under a scaffolding. Seeing the confused look on my face, the other girl, Rachel, giggled and said, "She doesn't want to get her hair wet."

I found out afterwards that Sarah cared so much about her hair because she'd spent hours flat-ironing it and didn't want the rain to "ruin" it. I was confused about why it was such a big deal. I asked Rachel why it mattered so much what her hair looked like. She just shrugged off the question. I assumed that spending so much energy to look pretty must be normal, and of course I wanted to be normal.

So, despite the fact that I already had stick-straight brown hair, I simply couldn't wait for the chance to flat-iron it. I thought to myself, "This is what it's going to take to make me attractive." Pretty soon I found myself in a constant haze of worry that I wasn't good enough.

Pressure from my friends wasn't the only reason I gave into mainstream culture's idea of what I should look like. As Jehovah's Witnesses, my parents had always warned me to resist the pressure of commercialism. During countless Jehovah's Witness meetings, the speaker would encourage everyone to reject modern fashion and dress conservatively.

But there were women at those meetings wearing pointy-toed shoes that cost hundreds of dollars. One man in the congregation even had a job doing interior design for Armani. Granted, this didn't account for all Jehovah's Witnesses, but in a religion that calls for modesty, these individuals seemed strangely placed. I was confused from a very early age by the mixed messages my religion seemed to be sending me.

So when I turned 13 and hit that typical rebellion phase, I figured the best way to rebel was to buy into mainstream consumer culture. I wanted to adhere to everything my religion wasn't, and I worked to become as much like the rest of the world as possible. I was a marketer's dream.

At the same time, all my waking hours outside of school were spent sitting in church, listening to lectures about how it was our duty to uphold some sort of Christian fantasy of what our appearance should be. My parents even started locking me in our apartment to keep me away from outside influences. Feeling constant pressure from two opposing worlds, I began functioning on autopilot and eventually did very little thinking for myself. At times I felt absolutely numb, and I don't doubt that for months at a time I was a complete zombie.

It was difficult to know anything about who I was or what I wanted, when there was such a steady flow of information from my parents telling me to button up my shirt and magazine ads telling me to unbutton it. As a result I had a very messy identity.

By the time I was 16, I was sick of it. No matter where I went outside my home, I felt constant pressure to be the conventionally pretty, innocent blonde or the typically skinny, edgy brunette with a cigarette. I was neurotic and unhappy about who I was becoming—a person who grew more shallow each day. I worried that if I didn't get out of New York, I'd lose the strength to resist the pressure from my parents, friends, and advertising.

A friend of mine from Denver, Colorado had been visiting New York that summer. Now that fall was approaching, she was going home and we met to say our goodbyes over bad pizza.

My parents were telling me to button up my shirt and magazine ads were telling me to unbutton it.

"It's a bummer you're leaving," I told her. "I can't stand it in New York, and now you won't even be here!" The thought of her leaving forced me to admit how unhappy I was with my friends and family, and with the person I'd become.

"You should come to Denver!" she said.

"There's no way I'd be able to," I laughed. "What an absurd idea."

"No! Really! You can stay with me!"

I thought about it a minute and wondered how my leaving would affect my family. Then I realized that I'd spent years going along with ideas that were not my own. If my mom and dad could find it in themselves to lock me inside our apartment in the name of God, I could stand to leave the state in the name of a chance.

I needed a cleansing period free from the pressures of religion and media. I had to reestablish my values, and my associates from birth to age 15 were not the people to be doing it with. I felt that they wouldn't care for me in the same way if I strayed from my flat-ironed hair and tight, ill-fitting Abercrombie clothing.

"OK," I finally said. "I'm gonna do it."

I told a close friend of mine about my situation and asked if he could buy me a ticket. Within half an hour he booked a one-way flight for me, and a week later I took a plane to Denver.

I felt amazing. I could finally get out for the first time in my life. I know not many people get the opportunity to ditch everything that makes them unhappy as easily as I did, but I was fortunate enough to have the chance to do it, so I took it. I ended up telling only a handful of people (I didn't tell my parents). I felt no remorse about leaving my family and friends, whose whole lives, I believed, were founded on being fake.

During my year in Denver as a runaway, my life was almost completely void of media. I didn't have a cell phone, TV, or radio. I didn't go to any malls or use the Internet. Slowly, I became a different person.

But it wasn't all these things that caused the change. The biggest influence was the people I met. Unlike my old friends in New York, my new friends were unmoved by ad culture. They made their own clothes and refused to support any big chain stores. They truly thought for themselves, instead of letting advertisements or religion dictate how they should be or dress.

I lived in a progressive community, where people cared about gender issues and took community work seriously. I lived in a house with five other people in their early 20s. My friends were punks. They were tattooed and pierced to all degrees. They had warm hearts and even warmer values, which they showed in their daily efforts to improve society. They worked for Food Not Bombs, providing free meals to the hungry, ran volunteer book collectives with activist, feminist, and anarchist literature, and also ran volunteer bike collectives, teaching anyone in the community about building bikes for free.

Eventually I got a job working at an art gallery and café, but until then, I had every one of my Denver friends to thank for always making sure that I was taken care of. Two of my friends even made me a bike. They came to my job one day and brought it along with them. That gesture was unlike anything anyone had ever done for me before. At that moment I realized people need to take care of each other, no matter what. I wanted to be able to alter people's lives like they had just altered mine.

One of my fondest Denver memories is when I went to a demonstration against sweatshops. The main speaker used to work in sweatshops and now leads rallies against Gap, Old Navy, Banana Republic, Abercrombie and Fitch, and other companies that use sweatshop labor.

She talked about the long hours and low pay, about pregnant women being fired because they couldn't complete their tasks on time. Hearing about what life is like working in a sweatshop was one of the most intense learning experiences of my life.

As I listened to her, I looked down and began to analyze everything I was wearing. I imagined someone working 40 hours straight, trying to meet a deadline of a hundred jeans per hour, and almost fainting from the heat of an overcrowded warehouse.

It's become easier to find happiness now that I have my own set of values.

After this experience it became simple for me to start rejecting commercialism. I became more aware of how advertisements and commercials are the economy's lifeblood—the average American views 3,000 ads a day, according to Jean Kilbourne's *Deadly Persuasion,* a book about how advertising influences and manipulates women and girls.

Without ads, how would people know just what kind of bed sheets to use? What kind of fabric softener to throw in to make the bed sheets soft? What type of clothes to wear, how worn and full of holes their $100 dollar jeans should be? What car to drive, liquor to drink, or cigarettes to smoke to attract the right kind of man or woman into those bed sheets? Without them, people would have to do just what I was learning to do in Denver—they would have to think for themselves.

I'd been taught that I needed to please everybody else. Now I saw that I needed to change the way I thought before I did any more damage to my self-esteem. I began to want to resist advertising not for the sake of "modesty," as my parents had taught me, but because of everything it represented—sweatshop labor, greed, and the manipulation of young minds.

Eventually, I decided to come back to New York because I wanted to finish high school. My parents, frightened by my running away, welcomed me back home with relief. But I was still worried about what awaited me there. In addition to my anxiety and sadness about leaving my friends in Denver, I feared that I wouldn't find any form of community once I arrived back in New York. I already suspected I'd have to cut all ties with my old New York friends.

My fears weren't unfounded. Even before I got back, word about me not shaving my legs spread like a wildfire among people I used to know. Needless to say, they didn't approve. And when I did come back, the first thing one of my old friends asked me was whether I'd seen how much weight a formerly chubby girlfriend of ours had lost. I just felt disgusted and said nothing. I haven't seen any of these people since. Instead, I've been working to find a group of friends who share my values.

Getting used to the constant onslaught of ads and commercialism I ran away from hasn't been easy either. I remember my first subway ride when I came back from Denver in August—my first subway ride in a year. The train howled and screeched into the station and the doors opened with that obnoxious "ding-dong," like mechanical harps welcoming me into a heaven of ads.

People parted to make a small space on the cluttered train for me. To my left, right, and even above my head on both walls of the train, there were advertisements for everything from vodka and storage space to Coach bags, Coca-Cola, and iPods. I noticed how white iPod headphone cords drooped from almost every other passenger's head, and Coach bags hung from their arms.

My anxiety mounted, and all I could say to myself was, "Here we go again." I'd have to learn how to cope with it, since I'd have to endure this form of transportation for as long as I lived in New York. Especially since my handmade bike had been stolen soon after I moved back.

It's become easier to find happiness now that I have my own set of values by which I live my life. My parents recognize this and have stopped pressuring me into rigid forms of religious worship. I've begun to openly criticize their methods and beliefs, and I think this had led them to back off.

One day, a few weeks after I returned, my mom asked me why I didn't shave my legs. So instead of telling her why I didn't, I decided to ask her why she did. Her reply was, "I think it's feminine to shave your legs." This response astounded me. She went on to say that women who don't shave their legs are usually lesbians. When I asked her if she would treat me differently if I were a lesbian, she said she didn't know.

But this time I didn't feel the need to run away from her pressure or anyone else's. I simply walked away. Thanks to Denver, I can gladly say that I am completely comfortable with who I am. Now I don't have to get on a plane to feel grounded.

The writer was in high school when she wrote this story.

Part 2: Family Matters

Mama Said...

What Our Mothers Tell Us About How a Girl Is Supposed to Behave

Wash the dishes. Mop the floor. This is how you broom under the bed. Keep your legs crossed—you're not a boy. Wear a dress, you would look so pretty. Why don't you stop wearing black? Why can't you be normal? You should go on a diet. Act like a lady.

When you grow up, get a good job so you can take care of yourself—that way you can use men and throw them away when you're done. Don't say, "So?"—that's rude. You need to learn how to use the washing machine so you can do the laundry.

When you get married, you'll need to know how to do these things so your husband won't leave you. Leave your hair loose—that's why your hair looks so ugly.

You're not gonna gain anymore weight, are you? Remember: when a girl goes to bed with all her boyfriends, she's a slut.

People get married to have children. Why don't you let your nails grow again? Your hands would look so pretty. Why do you only wear men's clothing? Why can't you be close with your brother and sisters the way I was?

You aren't as strong as your brother because he's a man and you're a woman. There are just some things you can't do because you're a girl. Why do you have to keep asking why your brother doesn't have to do this and you do—is it that you want to be a man now?

Why are you so violent? Can't you just behave? You can't get a tattoo because only men like those on the corner get tattoos — and you can get an infection!

Why can't you just act like a normal girl?! Why can't you just be happy the way you are?

—Clariza Sanchez

Wear a dress once in a while. Black cats bring bad luck, so get rid of it. Girls play with girls and boys play with boys. Girls play *like* girls and boys play *like* boys. You look so pretty in pink, you should wear it more often.

Don't put anything used to cut things on your bed. Always write on both sides on a sheet of paper, it'll last longer that way. You're not allowed to date until you're 15. You should learn how to cook—and fast. I don't want to see you with that junkie boyfriend of yours.

Those jeans are too big, one of these days you're going to trip and break your neck. Not everything is meant to be said. Let your hair grow long. For god's sake, you're not on the track team—stop running.

—Jessica Maissonet

Over the years my mom has told me: to wash the dishes because it would only be helping her; to pin up my hair, because when I don't I look really sleepy; to sit like a lady, or at least sit right, so I'll be respected as a lady; to dress neat so I'll be respected because of my neatness; that a lady's room should always be neat and not look like a garbage dump; that I should act like a lady in front of people, except when playing sports because she knows sports are sometimes dirty and are supposed to be fun; to respect myself first, because then other people will respect me too; that I couldn't act childish anymore because I am a grown up girl and have to act like one.

—Miranda Chung

You know you have to wash the dishes. Why? Because one day you will have a family. What are you gonna do when you have children—let the dishes pile to the sky?

You're gonna have to cook, you know. Why? Because when you get a man or a husband, you know how men like to eat. Men love to eat—look at your brothers and your father. Children have to be fed, you know. Speaking of children, one day you'll be a mother and I'll be a grandmother and children need to be watched at all times, especially babies, so start paying more attention to things now.

When you have babies, you can't be sleeping hard like that, you know. You say you don't want children now, but you'll change your mind. You're not gonna brush your hair down? Brush it down! Ladies wear dresses, if not every day, once in a while. That's only natural. Why don't you wear a dress today? Here, let me pat your hair down some.

—Faleisha Escort

Felicia Colombani

Our Parents' Rules:

Fair or Square?

By Miranda Chung

Almost all teen girls have to deal with rules—rules about where they can go and when they have to come home, what they can wear, and who they can date (if they can date at all).

"First thing, don't get pregnant."

"Do not date till you're 21 or until we're dead."

"No tight, tight clothes."

"Get good grades."

"Tell me where you're going."

"Get home by 9:30, 10 at the latest."

These are just a few of the things that girls I interviewed mentioned when I asked what basic rules their parents expect them to follow.

Almost everyone I talked to agreed that while some of their

parents' demands are reasonable, "sometimes they make up rules that are kind of hard to follow," as Johanna Peters, 16, put it. Most parents make rules because they want to protect their daughters and keep them out of trouble, and their kids realize this.

"New York is a dangerous city, a lot of things can happen to young girls," said Ruth Marantz, 15. "[My parents] just want to make sure I'm taking care of myself." Although she doesn't have a curfew, Ruth said her parents "expect me to call them, to tell them where I was, always. They're concerned about my safety. They'll make me take cabs late at night."

Others, like Faith Wallace, 16, think their parents are more concerned with controlling them than protecting them. "[My mother] doesn't want me to challenge her authority," she said. This frustrates Faith. "I think I should have the right to be left alone and make mistakes and make my own decisions, too," she said.

But even when girls think there are good reasons for their parents' rules, they don't always enjoy following them. Rachel Leung, 17, said her parents' rules include no dating until college, a 10 p.m. curfew, and the expectation that she'll get good grades. "I think they're doing this for my own good and so I won't mess up my life," Rachel said. But she also thinks her parents are too strict.

Rachel wishes she could stay out later because she thinks she's missing out on "all the fun and excitement." And she doesn't think she should have to wait until college to have a boyfriend. "If I found a nice person, I would date them but my parents wouldn't know," she said. But, basically, Rachel goes along with what her parents want. "I know I have no say in it," she said. "And I'm not the rebel type."

Johanna said her parents make rules "because they want me to have the best possible life I could have." But that doesn't mean she always follows them. Like Rachel, her curfew is "10 at the latest." She's not supposed to date or go to bars or clubs. But, unlike Rachel, "I rebel," Johanna said.

One time her parents "found out I was going out with some guy," she said. "I still kept going out with him. I felt kind of good because I got back at them." Sometimes she does things just to spite her parents, Johanna said. "Like before, when they didn't want guys calling, maybe I would give my number out more," she said.

The biggest fight Johanna ever had with her parents was over a guy calling. "They figured he was my boyfriend," she said. "They screamed at him. He turned out to be a classmate. I was very embarrassed. I went into my room and said I would never speak to them again. Eventually they came and apologized."

Guys are often a source of tension between girls and their parents—even when they are allowed to date. Faith said her mother has rules about the kind of guy she can go out with. "He has to be in school, he has to be doing something, he can't just be hanging with his boys on the street," she said.

Some girls think their parents are more concerned with controlling them than protecting them.

Mary Grace Colobong, 15, has gotten a similar message from her parents. They've told her, "Don't go out with lower status [guys] or gangsters," she said. Other girls said their folks just want to know who they're dating. "My dad wanted to meet my boyfriend," Ruth said. "Other than that [who I date] is basically not in their control."

Even though girls may not like these rules, they do see why they make some sense. But then there are the rules girls think are totally unreasonable—like telling them what they can and can't wear. Many girls said their parents won't let them wear things that are too tight, too revealing, or too sloppy, and these are among the things they get most upset about.

"I don't think it's a parent's place to tell you how to dress," said Vanessa Ho, 17. Vanessa said her parents can "express their opinions" about her clothes but they "can't tell me what I can and can't wear."

But many parents do think it is their right to tell their daughters how to dress.

"My mom will say, 'You can't wear that' and I say, 'Why?' and she says, 'It's too tight,'" said Faith.

Makeda Benjamin, 17, said, "My mother doesn't let me show my stomach or wear tight, tight clothes, but my father doesn't really mind." Makeda said that last summer when she wore something her mother didn't like, her mom "didn't make me take the clothes off but she would complain and get real mad." Makeda said that, in the end, "I would just change my mind and go with her way."

But a lot of times, girls refuse to go with their parents' way. If there's something they really want to do, they'll go ahead and do it, even if their parents have said no. "I think they're unfair at times," Vanessa said. "I kind of just ignore them and do it anyway." Or, she said, "I talk to them and say, 'Look, this is unfair' and they let me do what I want to do."

One time Faith's mother told her she couldn't go to a party. "But I went to a friend's house and went anyway. [My mom] found out from calling my friend's house," Faith said. "When I got home, I just went to my room, slept late and came out in the morning. She just said, 'I'm very disappointed in you, if you ever do that again I'm going to come down there in my slippers and rollers in my hair.' " Afterwards, Faith regretted what she had done. "I felt really bad, I felt guilty," she said. "I was like, I can't believe I did that."

Even Ruth, who described her parents as "very easy going," and said, "they trust me so I can deal with the rules," has disobeyed on occasion. "I've sneaked out of the house before," she said. Afterwards, she felt "half happy with myself and half guilty."

The girls I interviewed usually felt bad about breaking the rules. Most said they try to talk to their parents and convince them to change rules that they find too strict. "I protest, I voice my opinion," Ruth said. "It doesn't hurt just to talk things out."

Mary Grace agreed. "Like a suggestion I made about dating and what age—they took it pretty seriously."

But most of the girls also felt that there were times when their parents are just being unreasonable. "The information they give me is [from] like 20 million years ago," said Mary Grace. "This is the 21st century and things are different."

Faith disagrees about parents being so out of touch. She thinks the real reason parents are sometimes hard on their kids is because they weren't perfect angels when they were teenagers and they don't want their children to repeat their mistakes. "I think our parents know what they were doing at 16 and they don't want us to do that," Faith said.

Miranda was 17 when she wrote this story. She graduated high school, worked as a medical technician, and attended SUNY Stony Brook, majoring in biology.

Beatrice Bass

House Arrest

By Anonymous

My father died four years ago, when I was 14. Since then, my older brother has taken control of my life. This is the worst thing that's ever happened to me.

My brother is only one year older than me, but after my father's death, the rest of the family said that he had to take the place of my dad. Now my mom listens to him and gives him whatever he wants because he is her favorite. The two of them can talk about anything. If my brother has a girlfriend or gets into any trouble, he will talk to my mom about it.

But if I try to talk to her about certain things—like if I want to go out with my friends or have a boyfriend—she just gets mad. My brother is allowed to party, hang out with friends, and go on dates. I am not.

It was different when my dad was alive. He trusted me and I

could talk to him about anything. He always helped me when I was in trouble and always made me feel important.

My brother is even worse than my mother—overprotective and controlling. He is always telling me what to do. I can't wear short clothes. I can't talk on the phone longer than 15 minutes because he will say, "I'm not paying the bill." If I go to the gym in the evening, I have to come home no later than 9 p.m. If I am hanging out with my friend right in front of our house, he will tell me to come inside. He is always telling me, "If you don't do what I say, you have to leave the house."

My family is from Guyana and has old-fashioned ways. They believe that if a girl wears short clothes, or hangs out with guys, or goes to clubs, she is disgracing the family. They believe that if you are going out with a guy, he has to become your husband—no dating lots of different guys before you get married. Even when I was living back in Guyana, I was never allowed to go out shopping by myself or wear jeans or bring friends to my house.

These things didn't bother me when I was in school because I was thinking of my studies. But when I started working, at age 16, that changed. I started to rebel. I would go out by myself and invite my friends to my house. But my mom and brother always made comments like, "Why are you bringing your friend over? Why can't you keep by yourself?"

Having no freedom was hard to take when I was 16 in Guyana. Now that I am 18 and living in New York City, it's unbearable. In Guyana, some girls cannot leave their parents' house until they are married, but in New York it is different. I see that girls my age are allowed to do anything, like go to clubs and hang out late at night.

But my mother and brother want my life to consist of just school and work. They think that will keep me from doing anything "wrong," like having a boyfriend or hanging out with friends or drinking or getting into fights. They want me to always wear long dresses or jeans, never a miniskirt. In my free time, they want me to stay home, watching TV or reading. I can't stand it. I want to have a social life. "All work and no play makes Jack a dull boy," as the old saying goes.

My mom says, "When you get married, you can do what you want or what your husband allows you to do." But I don't want to wait that long to have a good time.

Compared to me, my friends are having a wonderful life. When I tell friends what I am going through, they say, "You got a heart to take it." Every weekend they ask me if I am going out with them. When I refuse because my family won't allow it, they get mad at me.

It's hard to keep friends when you are not allowed to go out at night. And it's impossible to have a boyfriend. I meet a lot of guys, but the relationships don't last because I cannot go out on dates.

Even though I don't do anything wrong, my mother and brother treat me like I do. I am sick of being a good girl and not getting any reward for it, so sometimes I break the rules. I buy short clothes and hide them under my bed so my mom won't find them, and then I wear them to school. I make sure I get home early, before my mother and brother. Or I wear them when I work nights because they're usually asleep by the time I get home. So far I haven't gotten caught, but if I ever was, I know my mother would throw all my short clothes away.

My brother is allowed to party, hang out with friends, and go on dates. I am not.

My brother and I are always getting into arguments because I try to fight for my rights. I get mad and tell him that he doesn't have any right to control me. Then he gets mad.

Sometimes he hits me, but I told him I'm going to call the police the next time he does that. Other times he says he is going to move out and live by himself. When he says that, my mom gets mad at me and says, "I prefer you leave because you are causing the problem."

My mom always takes my brother's side. He was her first child and she likes him more than me. Sometimes she tells me that I came into this world by mistake because she was not planning to have another baby. Sometimes I wish I wasn't born, because what is the use of living when you cannot have any fun? I try to occupy my time with working, going to school and going to the gym, so I don't have to spend much time at home.

Sometimes I feel like running away because my family makes my life miserable if I don't do what they say. But I don't want to leave the house now because I am going to school full-time and working part-time. The money I make is enough to buy my clothes and lunch, but it's not enough to pay rent.

I wish my father were alive. I don't feel the same without him. I was Daddy's girl. I could tell him when I was in trouble and he would give me advice. He always had faith in me and said I would be a better person than my brother. If he were here, I think my life would be completely different.

I remember when I was 13 a guy wrote me a love letter. My mother found it and she started hitting me. Then my father came in and rescued me. I had already told him about the guy and he said having a boyfriend or someone close was OK, as long as there was no hugging or kissing. He said I should know myself and be careful. I still broke up with the boy who wrote me the letter because my mom told me that if I continued the relationship, she would take me out of school.

My mother wants me to wait until I get married to have a life, but that's not the right solution for me.

I know that even if my father was alive, I wouldn't always get my way. There would be disagreements between my parents because my father would want to allow me to do certain things and my mom would not. He might not always win the argument, but at least I would have someone who listened to me and took my side. And that would make all the difference in the world.

But I have to deal with the situation as it is. The fact that I have rebelled and argued with my mother and brother over the rules I consider unfair has made things a little better. Now at least they let me go shopping by myself and I can have my friends visit my house. If I hadn't fought them, I would still be shopping with my mom and only seeing my friends at school. I feel better because I have gotten them to give up a little of their control over me.

Right now though, what I really want to do is start college so I can move out of my house. (Even though I finished high school in Guyana, I have to do the GED over here, so that I can go to college.) I will finish my GED in December, and I will apply to college for the spring semester. I want to live in a dorm, so I can go to parties and hang out with friends and have a social life. I know my mom will be mad at me if I leave home to live in a dorm, but I don't care.

My mother wants me to wait until I get married to have a life, but that's not the right solution for me. Before I get married, I want to travel, party, have fun with friends, and get a good job. Most of all, I want to be in control of my life and have the freedom to make decisions for myself.

The author was in high school when she wrote this story.

University of Kitchen?

By Orubba Almansouri

"We're halfway through the summer. Are we going to New York or what?" I asked my older sister Yasmin. She had come to visit us at our house back in my country, Yemen. We were in the room we'd shared until she got married and moved away.

"Do you really want to go?" she replied, opening the Kit Kat bar she had in her hand.

"Yes and no," I answered as I lay down on my bed. "I want to stay here for you and all our extended family, but I also want to see Dad and New York City."

"What's the rush, then? It's not like you're going to school when you get there," she said.

In my family, most men believe that the best place for a woman is in the house and the best job for us women is to cook, clean and raise a family. Many girls in my family—including

Yasmin—stop going to school before high school, and none have gone to college. Girls live with their families until they are 15 or a little older, then it's time to say goodbye to being single and hello to marriage.

My religion (Islam) is not against girls being educated. In fact our Prophet Mohammed, may peace be upon him, said that we should seek education even if we have to go to China for it. The problem isn't my culture either, since many Yemeni girls are educated and have jobs. Where my family's tradition came from, I don't know. But so far, no one has broken it.

I never imagined my destiny would be any different. In my country I was an excellent student and teachers loved me. In 7th grade, I was first in my class. They put my name in big letters on a piece of paper and hung it up in the main hallway. I felt so proud of myself.

I didn't mind leaving school at any time, though, because I knew the path girls in my family followed and I didn't expect anything else. When we came to the United States the first time (when I was 5—we stayed for a few years), my older sisters were teenagers and they didn't get a chance to go to school, even though they really wanted to go and learn English. So when I was 14 years old and I heard that we were moving back to the US, I figured I wouldn't be going to school anymore.

Then we got to New York, and my dad announced he was planning to enroll my sister Lebeya and me in school. I was surprised. From what I used to see on TV, American high schools were another planet compared to schools in Yemen. I wasn't used to going to school with boys, or talking to them. In fact, I was a little worried: I'd heard that many Yemeni students who go to American high schools start to do what the other kids are doing, like having relationships and even drinking, neither of which is allowed by my religion. I'd expected my dad would want to keep my sister and me away from this environment. (My mom wants us to be educated, as she never had the chance to be, but like most Yemeni women she follows her husband's decisions.)

But my dad was determined. When my oldest sisters didn't go to school in New York, that affected their lives and his. They couldn't go out alone because they didn't understand English and couldn't communicate. My dad had to translate for them at doctors' appointments. When we moved to New York, he said putting my sister and me in school would help us become independent so we could help ourselves when necessary.

For my part, I decided that since I had the chance to go to school, I would definitely take it. Today my sisters are both married and have children sweet as honey, but they still wish they had gone to school here and learned to speak English. I saw from my sisters' experience that education was the best thing for me, and I felt that going to school might be fun and a way to get out of the house. I had no idea what it would become to me.

While we were getting records and report cards sent from Yemen to New York so my sister and I could enroll here, the men in my extended family started telling my dad that we would get ourselves into trouble and hurt the family's reputation. They thought that high school in America would Americanize us, causing us to drop the traditions we'd been learning our entire lives and pick up others.

The truth is that there is always a question mark over my future.

One day my dad was on the phone with one of my cousins and I heard some of my dad's replies. (It's not my fault he thought that I was sleeping when I wasn't.) They went like this:

"They are my daughters and I have raised them right. I know what is good for them."

"It's none of your business."

"I don't care what they say, I have listened to you guys once and I won't make that mistake again."

After I heard that, I was saying to myself, "Way to go, Dad!" I saw my father as someone who is ready to make a change and someone who really cares about his daughters' education; I saw him in a way that made me feel proud to be the daughter of Ali Almansouri. I knew that my dad had put all his trust in us and this made me want to be on my best behavior.

My first day at Brooklyn International High School was scary because I was starting 9th grade at the end of September and I was the new girl. I felt lonely at first, but luckily my English was OK from living here as a kid. By second period I'd talked to two Hispanic girls and we became friends. My teachers were so nice to me; they helped me when I needed help and they always asked me how I was doing. I began to love school once again. I worked hard and got excellent grades. My classmates started telling me, "You're so smart."

I don't believe that I'm as smart as they say, but I do believe that I am clever. Because I did well, ideas of actually graduating started coming into my head. My love for school grew, especially when I learned new things, went on trips or met new friends.

"You know that I will be the first girl from our family to actually go to college," I said one day to my sisters and a group of other girls, while we were sitting together talking.

"Yeah, and you'll go to the University of Kitchen," my younger cousin said.

"And earn your cooking degree," my sister added.

Then they all started laughing, including me. "You'll see when I become the first Almansouri girl to go to college and break the 'girls don't go to college' rule," I said. "You'll see what I will do."

The truth is, though, that there is always a question mark over my future. In spite of the things I overheard my dad say on the phone, his decisions about my future are not all made yet. My dad doesn't really follow up on my schoolwork, and when opportunities come up—like leadership programs, after-school activities or writing for Youth Communication—it's not easily that he lets me participate.

I think that even though he put me in school, sometimes he still thinks the way other men in my family do. This worries me, because it makes me think he may not allow me to finish the path that he let me start. However, if I give him a great speech about why he should let me do some extracurricular thing, and if I'm persistent, he usually gives in. I think that when I put it in his head that I can benefit a lot from these things, he sees it, and that gives me hope for the future.

My being allowed to finish high school and go to college depends on two people: Dad and me. I will never disobey him because he is everything to me. My basic hope is that we don't go back to Yemen before I graduate from high school. Then, if my dad lets me, I'd prefer to put off marriage until I am settled in college.

What will actually happen, I don't know. My dad hasn't told me what he's thinking. Even though I hate not knowing what's going to be next, in another way I don't want the topic to come up yet. I'm afraid of the answer I'll get, in case it's a "no." Anyway, as they say, you have to walk up the ladder step by step or you'll fall down.

When I'm feeling hopeful, I think my dad will let me go to college. I want to attend a good one like Columbia University, major in English or journalism and also study biology. I see my future as a finishing line with red and white stripes, and I see myself crossing the line, then getting my prize—in other words, working in a career and feeling true power and independence. I also want to feel useful to the world and to people around me. I want to learn more and be an educated person.

Sometimes, though, I feel that everything I do is for no reason and that I will never be able to go to college or even finish high school. I worry that if I do graduate from high school, my dad will say, "I already let you finish high school and we don't have women who go to college in this family." I worry about the pressure that will be on him if he does let me go to college. Our family made such a big deal about us going to high school, I can't imagine what they would say about college.

When I hear things like, "Look—girls your age are getting married and soon it will be your turn," those comments are like rockets landing in my ears. I find a place to be alone and think to myself, "All this hard work, these top grades, these compliments, for what? For me to remember when I'm seasoning the soup. Why did they put me in the race when I had no interest in participating? They put the idea in my head, made me like it and actually work toward something—all so that when I reach the finish line they'll tell me I can't cross it."

When I'm feeling hopeful, I think my dad will let me go to college.

I imagine watching others cross the line without me, and hunt myself down for all the time I spent dreaming of things I want to accomplish. "Maybe it's not time, Orubba," I think. "Maybe the girl that will break your family's record hasn't been born yet."

With that I cry myself to sleep. Sometimes I even have nightmares about not finishing high school. A lot of people think that it's no big deal; I'll get married and my husband will give me everything I need. But that's not enough for me because I want my life to have different flavors and taste them all, not just repeat the same flavor over and over every day. I also want to feel that I'm prepared if something happens to my husband. How will I feed my children? I want to have a weapon in my hand and education is one weapon that never hurts anyone, but actually helps.

In Yemen, I always thought that going to college was a good thing for girls, but I didn't feel envious of the girls from other families who could go. Since I came to the US, though, I have been thinking more about my future and I want more out of life. Because I see college as a possibility for me, but not a sure thing, today I feel envious toward Yemeni girls who know they can go to college.

Sometimes I get mad that my family keeps on pushing boys

to go to college, even though most of them don't have any interest, while some of us girls are ready to work for it and never get a chance. Other times, I tell myself that whatever education I end up with is better than nothing. I'm even a little afraid of going to college in case I fail. I'm torn between two things, but the tear is not straight down the middle. I'm happy that my obsession with success is greater than my worries.

Now I'm a junior, my grades are still excellent, and my desire to live my dream is greater than ever. I agree with some of my family's traditions, like girls not going out alone and not sleeping at anyone's house outside the family. But the education issue is too much. If they give all us girls a chance and support us, we can help our family reach higher than ever before. If I go to college, I'll open a path and be a role model for future generations of girls in the family, teaching them not to give up.

If my father's decision is for me to go to college, he will raise his head high and tell everyone who wanted to stand in my way that they were wrong; that he is happy and proud that he gave us a chance that a lot of parents in my family took away from their girls. I want him to be really pleased with what I accomplish.

Everything I become will be because of the trust he gave me. I will keep my religion and my traditions, but I will follow my dreams as long as I know that what I'm doing is right. I have no problem with cooking and cleaning, as long as it is a side order with my dream. But if my dad doesn't support my dream, then everything that I have planned for won't be. That's what causes me nightmares instead of dreams.

Orubba was 16 when she wrote this story.

Part 3: How Do We Look?

Shaun Shishido

Fashion Un-Conscious

By Nadishia Forbes

Back home in Jamaica, I never really worried about whether my clothes matched. At school, the only thing that mattered was how clean my uniform was and whether it was ironed. When I went to visit my friends, I would just put on a couple of freshly washed pieces of clothing without even thinking about how they looked.

We were kids—our friendships were not based on appearance; we just liked to run around and have fun. It didn't matter if our braided hair was pointing in all directions and our blouses and skirts had some buttons missing, or if we were barefoot and covered in red dirt. I never experienced being judged because of the way I dressed—until I came to the U.S. The first time it happened was on my first day of junior high school, which was also my first day in an American school.

I was a little scared that day, mainly because of the new environment. Walking down the hall, I felt very self-conscious, so I turned around to get a better look at my classmates.

Two girls were staring at me, whispering and giggling. I stopped and waited for them to pass, but they said to go ahead, so I did. They continued looking at me, but I didn't say anything because I didn't know how to respond.

Even though I couldn't hear their conversation, I assumed it had something to do with the way I was dressed. They were wearing designer jeans, the latest name brand sneakers, and outfits that matched. Plus, they had their hair permed.

I never experienced being judged because of the way I dressed—until I came to the U.S.

I was wearing a pink and black plaid jumper with two straps in front, a blue, red, and white striped long-sleeved blouse, thick black stockings, and brown shoes. And I just had big braids in my hair, because my grandmother didn't want me to perm it, and that was fine with me.

When I got to my first period class, a couple or more of my classmates pointed out my shoes or clothes to their friends and laughed. Some of them even started throwing papers in my direction.

I looked different than everyone else and that was a big problem. When you start junior high, the pressure to fit in and gain respect is intense. The kids who made fun of me were popular—partly because their designer clothes made them seem cool. My clothes made me stand out and gave the others an excuse to pick on me.

I was the perfect target and it wasn't just because of the way I dressed. I was in a new environment and that made me feel scared and insecure. I was like a fish outside its water bowl. My classmates saw that I was in a position of weakness and wouldn't stand up for myself. They took advantage of that.

Almost every day, I would be greeted with giggles, pointing, and other demonstrations of their disapproval. For a long time, I didn't have any friends to back me up and the teacher did nothing to control the students. I felt like everyone was against me, like no one was on my side. Two girls named Luvia and Nefertiti were the main sources of my torment. They would put "kick me" signs on my back, throw papers at me and make fun of my clothes.

For the first time in my life, I didn't want to go to school. When I got home each day, I would cry and complain to my grandmother about what was happening, but she was too busy to do anything about it. Sometimes she would say, "Ignore them," or tell me to tell their mothers. Then she would force me to go back to school. She never really understood how hurt and depressed I was.

I would go to school each day with my heart pounding. I hardly paid attention and I never really learned anything. It was hard to concentrate on my schoolwork. The other students were very disruptive. Because I was quiet, the teacher always pointed me out as an example to the rest of the class and that made it worse for me because I was now considered the teacher's pet.

To take my mind off the fact that I might end up in a fight any minute, I'd bring a thick romance novel to school and just sit in class and read all day. Instead of focusing on learning like I should have, I focused on surviving.

I did make one friend that year. Her name was Tina. She was really friendly and we had a couple of things in common. We were both from Jamaica, but Tina had been here for five years. We both had strict families. Tina wore the latest styles of name brand clothing, just like Luvia and Nefertiti, but unlike them, she never judged me for the way I dressed.

Tina would take up for me when the others were picking on me. She would tell them to leave me alone and always tried to help me out. One time, Luvia tried to spite Tina by saying that Tina and I were sisters. Later that day, I wrote a poem to Tina, titled, "You're Like a Sister," and she liked it.

Having Tina as a friend made the days more bearable because I was not entirely alone. But it didn't make much of a difference in terms of how I was treated by the other kids. In fact, it didn't make any difference at all.

Around the middle of the school term, I started to think that maybe if I dressed like the rest of them, they wouldn't bother me so much. I hadn't made any effort to fit in sooner because I was stubborn. But I was tired of having people treat me like I was beneath them.

One day, I went to school wearing yellow socks and a yellow blouse with a black skirt. Right at the beginning of class, Nefertiti showed Luvia my socks and said, "What are you doing?" with a smirk. It was as if she was saying, "No matter what you do, you won't look as good as us." Not knowing what to say, I turned my back, feeling a little defeated. I went back to wearing my usual outfits.

It was as if she was saying, "No matter what you do, you won't look as good as us."

A month or two later, my uncle's girlfriend gave me a pair of trendy sneakers. I wore them to school and I have to admit they gave me a little confidence. I actually felt some enthusiasm, thinking that probably I would get a little acceptance with my new shoes. When I got to school, one kid actually announced to the class that I had on name brand sneakers. Everyone looked, but I didn't feel any more accepted by my peers than I had before.

No matter what I did, they wouldn't let up. Luvia, in particular, was always throwing things at me or hitting me. I never started anything with her; she was always coming after me. Then the kids she hung around with would tell her how bad she was.

One day in the spring, she was in the hallway surrounded by her friends when I passed by. When she saw me, she hit me. I didn't want to fight, so I continued to walk, as I usually did. But for some reason on that day, I couldn't take it anymore. I decided it had to stop.

So when I saw Luvia in the cafeteria, I went up to her and slapped her face. The next thing I knew, I was on the floor. Luvia was much bigger than me so it wasn't much of a surprise when I lost the fight.

Later that day, Luvia and her friends came up to me. She was very upset and kept staring at me, but she didn't say anything. I went home early.

That night, I told my father how these two girls had been giving me a hard time. He decided to take a day off from work and come to school with me and make a complaint. We went to the counselor's office. She called in Luvia, sat the two of us down, and asked about the fight and about what was going on between us. Then she talked to us for a while.

I didn't really hear what the counselor was saying. I was too busy staring at Luvia and wondering what she thought about all this and what the other kids would think when they heard about it. After my father left, I went back to class. Everyone was looking at me.

After that, Luvia didn't hit me or throw things at me anymore but she and her friends still gave me dirty looks.

When I finally finished 7th grade, I had the greatest summer of my life—simply because I had survived. I would stay home most of the time watching TV, without anyone tormenting me.

In 8th grade, things got better. Everyone started to settle in and feel more comfortable. They let down some of their guard, which made for a less hostile environment. My classmates stopped making fun of my clothes. I didn't really change the way I dressed, but I stopped wearing certain things—like skirts and dresses that made me look like I was going to church.

I got the chance to make more friends because everyone was friendlier. When I got the chance to know my classmates, I was surprised. They weren't really bad people. And Luvia and Nefertiti weren't in my class anymore, which made everything much easier for me. I didn't dread going to school anymore.

Seventh grade was a difficult year, but I got through it, I think because I knew it wouldn't always be that way and I was determined to succeed. My family and Tina did their best to help me, but the strength I had inside came from my faith in God. The experience taught me never to judge people by appearance. I never tease anyone because of what they wear or how they look. I've also got the best of friends because I didn't pick them based on how they look, but by getting to know them as individuals.

After 7th grade, I only saw Nefertiti and Luvia occasionally. But, during graduation rehearsal, I saw Luvia giggling and whispering to her friend and I could tell they were talking about me.

It didn't bother me at all. Knowing that this was the end of 8th grade and junior high and that I would never have to see them again, I gave them a big smile. And that wiped the smile off Luvia's face. I think she was disappointed because I wasn't upset. She no longer had any power over me. I turned around feeling happy and triumphant.

I'm in 11th grade now and I don't get teased anymore, even though I still dress pretty much the same way. I have friends now. I know that I'm smart and will be successful one day. But the difficulty I went through in 7th grade still has an effect on me.

Sometimes, when I walk in front of the class, I feel self-conscious about my appearance. Sometimes, when I hear someone laughing, I still think they're laughing at me.

Nadishia was 17 when she wrote this story.
She later joined the Army.

YC Art Dept.

The Identity Experiment

By Lily Mai

One morning last month, I curled my hair and tied a bit of it back to show my face. I also wore an excessive amount of black eyeliner and dark eye shadow for a "smoky eyes" look. I wore my mother's black shoes with tight blue jeans and a tight black T-shirt to show off my black hair. I thought I looked good and I felt confident.

When I got to school, I saw my good friend in the hallway. She looked at me and said, "I haven't seen you in two weeks and you look good! Wow." I told her I wanted the "dress to kill" look.

She smiled at me, looked me up and down, nodded her head and said, "Yeah, you're definitely dressed to kill."

Every time I went to the bathroom to check my eye makeup, I couldn't help but think about my freshman year and how I never would've done something like this. Back then, I always wore plain clothing. I had fuzzy hair in a ponytail and I didn't use gel or hair spray to make it less puffy. I looked like the stereotypical smart, quiet Chinese girl.

Recently I've started changing—tweezing my eyebrows, styling my hair. But I don't usually wear makeup or shoes with heels, and I was surprised at how much people noticed the change. Later that day, a guy in the hallway looked me in the face and said, "Hey, how you doing, Miss?" I was surprised because that doesn't often happen to me.

When I walked into class, a classmate looked me up and down with a "What's the occasion?" look. Before I knew it, the whole class was saying things like, "What are you doing after school?" and, "Do you have a date?"

All I'd done was add eye makeup and some tight jeans, and I felt completely different.

I just blushed and looked away. I didn't want to be the center of the attention. I knew I looked good, but to me it wasn't something to talk or brag about. It was more of an inside kind of feeling for me, a confidence that I'd longed to feel all through high school.

It was amazing. All I'd done was add eye makeup and some tight jeans, and I felt completely different. And other people saw me completely differently, too.

I wondered, "How much does our appearance affect how people perceive us and how we feel about ourselves?" If I got this big a reaction from a little eye shadow, what if I looked completely different? Would people react differently? Would I feel different? I decided to do an experiment to figure out just how much our appearance can shape how we think of ourselves.

I planned to try out different identities on different days—goth, clubber, hip-hop, and my normal look—to see if people would react differently. I'd take the same route home each day and stop at the same corner deli. The only difference would be my appearance. That way I could be sure that anything I was feeling, and any reactions I got, would be based on how I looked.

The next day, I came to the Youth Communication office and a goth writer helped me dress like her. I wore a black lace collar, black Converse sneakers, huge baggy black pants with gold zippers everywhere, a spiked belt, and silver chains wrapped around my hips. I also wore three huge necklaces, including a heavy back cross on a chain. I wore a massive amount of black makeup—eyeliner, eye shadow, even black lipstick and nail polish. I drew a black star on the bottom of my left eye to enhance the dark look.

When I looked at myself in the mirror, I saw myself as the same person, just wearing a different outfit. I didn't feel different until I was out in public. As I walked along 34th Street, a middle-aged guy looked at me. After we crossed paths, he turned his head and continued to stare. I knew from his eyes that he wasn't looking at me because I was beautiful, but because I looked different.

More heads turned as I continued down 34th Street, and I could see people giving me this "what-the-hell-was-she-thinking" look. Their stares seemed to say I wasn't like them and I didn't belong in this society. I was starting to hate being dressed like this.

After being stared at and even laughed at on the train home, my stomach felt queasy and I was crying inside. I wanted to get out of this outfit now. I didn't want to look like this anymore. I couldn't handle the stress.

I have friends who are goth and they tell me that people often give them stares and they don't care at all. Their attitude is "screw what everyone thinks—normal people suck."

I think these friends dress goth because it's a reflection of who they are, but I don't fully understand it because I'm not like that. I found that I hated the attention. I also think for me it was a little different because I'm Chinese and people aren't used to seeing a Chinese girl dressed this way.

That evening, I went to a corner deli near my friend's house in Harlem. I'd gone there the day before in my "girly" heels and tight jeans, and the deli guy had given me a horny, turned-on look. But this time he didn't pay any attention to me. He wasn't even looking at me as I bought my M&Ms. I knew right then that people do treat you differently depending on how you dress.

I was relieved to get home that night. Though I liked the comfort of the black baggy pants, I hated people's mean reactions and that they couldn't just accept my style. This was not an identity I'd try again.

For my next outfit, I went for a "downtown, clubbing in the Village" look. After my miserable goth experience, I was excited to look feminine again. I was ready to walk around in my short skirt and I looked forward to people's reactions.

As I was applying my makeup, I thought about how long it was taking me. And even though I don't normally like the idea of being hit on, I found myself thinking, "Someone has to hit on me—all this hard work has to pay off!" I had no idea what I was in for.

Dressed in a green top, a gauzy black miniskirt, and heeled ankle boots, I felt so naked. More naked than I'd ever felt in my entire life. Walking to the subway was embarrassing and I wanted to walk faster to get away, but I couldn't. Not in these shoes. I felt everyone's eyes on my bare legs. I wished I'd brought a pair of jeans with me to hide my legs.

In the subway station, a teenager said to me, "Hey Sweetie," and I felt his eyes roam all over my body. I actually smiled in my head because he was the first to really say something about my outfit, and I found it flattering.

But when I got out of the train, a grown man in his 30s looked at me from head to toe and said, "Mmmm," like I was food and it looked delicious. As I made my way across the street, a man wearing a huge fur coat and handing out fliers said, "Nice legs." I was starting to wish I'd never walked out of the house like this.

As the day went on, I found that I didn't like the attention after all. I felt like my butt was hanging out of my skirt. I felt like people thought I was a slut or a hooker and I hated looking like one. I got comments from three more guys (all grown men) in one block. A guy in a white van even stopped and waved for me to come over to him.

After a while I put on this sad, long, depressed face so people would leave me alone and not think of me as a slut. I told myself, "I'm returning this skirt tomorrow." When I stopped to buy a soda, a man coming out of the store said, "Look at you looking all sexy." In the store, another man said that I had "this innocent face that burns all." I said thank you because I thought it was a compliment, but after I left I wasn't so sure.

This experience has confirmed my idea that we're judged immediately by what we wear.

Later, I went into that same corner deli where I'd gone the previous two days. This time, the guy behind the deli counter (who'd looked at me hungrily in my girly outfit and ignored me in my goth outfit) looked at me from head to toe as if disgusted. He gave me a dirty look like I was a prostitute. I couldn't wait to get home and change into a pair of jeans.

What surprised me most about dressing in this outfit was that I liked it, at least at first. I liked that it made me feel—and I hate to admit this—pretty inside because of the compliments I got. But after a while, the looks from people on the street made me feel like I was a tramp.

For my "hip-hop" outfit, I wore a huge, sleeveless basketball jersey and a flat-brimmed baseball cap, both of which I borrowed from my boyfriend. The jersey was like a dress on me, but I tucked the bottom into my jeans, and with my puffy black down jacket over it, it wasn't too noticeable.

But I felt miserable because I thought I looked boyish. I hated the hugeness of the shirt. And I hate wearing anything on my head because I wear glasses. The cap kept falling on my glasses, which made my glasses keep falling down my face. But most of all, I felt I looked like a fake, trying to look cool.

When I walked the same streets as I had in all my other outfits, the looks I got weren't surprising. People's eyes clung to my face until I passed them, and girls gave me this weird "who is she trying to be, dressing that way" look.

When I was in the deli, a teenage girl looked me up and down and breathed in my entire outfit. I could tell she thought I was trying too hard to fit in and that made me feel angry. Plus, I felt like I was trying too hard too, and it was annoying. Even the deli guy looked at me from head to toe with a smirk on his face.

At the end of the day, there was nothing I liked about my hip-hop outfit. I didn't look or feel pretty. The shirt was too long, the cap was huge on my small head and the entire look was way out of my league. I'd never wear it again.

After that experience, it was a relief to dress as my regular self the next day. I wore a plain black T-shirt and jeans, with no makeup or accessories. I liked the simplicity of the outfit. I didn't have to worry about whether my eyeliner was smudged or if my earrings went with my outfit or if my hair looked right. I felt so laid back and relaxed, like this was the real me. The quiet, innocent me.

And not surprisingly, I didn't get any reactions the whole day. No looks or "Hey Sweetie" or muttering. It was as if they didn't see me at all. But I saw the real me in that outfit, and I liked it. I'm just another ordinary-looking girl, and I'm happy with that.

This whole experience has taught me a couple of things. It confirmed my idea that we're judged immediately by what we wear. Our clothes are windows into our identities. When strangers see us, they make assumptions about who we are based on our appearance, and they react accordingly.

I also learned how much my feelings about myself are based on other people's reactions. In the goth outfit, I didn't feel one bit different until I went outside. When people started staring and laughing, it really hurt and made me want to take off the outfit right away.

And when I wore the short skirt, I felt flattered by the compliments I got. I'd never thought I was pretty, but those reactions gave me a little hope that I might not be bad looking after all. At the same time, when people looked at me like I was a slut, I felt naked and uncomfortable.

When I look in the mirror, I want to see myself in what I wear, and I want other people to see who I am. This experiment gave me a better idea of who that is. I found that I was afraid to wear outfits like goth and hip-hop, but I was excited about wearing the girly outfits. Maybe that's who I am—maybe I'm more of a girly girl than I'd thought.

I think I never admitted that to myself before because I was ashamed of it. I didn't want to be one of those girls who has to buy the latest trends and cries when she breaks a nail. But I actually like wearing girly clothes and a little makeup, and I like getting compliments (as long as they're from guys my age).

I like feeling comfortable too, though. For now, I'll probably keep my same look and just wear a little eye makeup occasionally, and maybe even a skirt. One that covers my legs though—I've already returned the miniskirt.

Lily was 17 when she wrote this story. After high school, she went to Brooklyn College.

Suits Me

By Jen Butler

In my short life, I've worn many different styles of clothes.

My first: the same suit that everyone starts out with, my birthday suit. Believe it or not, I spent a lot of time in that famous suit. (My 'rents, like all parents, took a lot of pictures of me like that. Why, I have no idea.) I guess I didn't mind, even though I looked kind of goofy. Still, I'm very glad that I don't have to go around naked anymore.

My second suit was one of those footie thingies, ya know, the kind that covers the hands and feet of babies. I liked mine, it was warm and fuzzy, but I just couldn't stand the whole pink thing. Yuck! A couple of months later came those stupid little frilly dresses. Eww, I usually only wore those when I had to go to the darn baby-sitter or out somewhere.

One of the most horrible dresses that I had to wear was this pink frilly one. Like I said, I really don't like pink. I guess because it is usually associated with little girls being proper. Pink is about sitting down to have tea with Barbie and stuffed little animals. And not running around the house, and not playing in mud, and not playing "Thundercats."

Besides being pink, this dress had puffy arms and a satin bow and was made out of some scratchy material. It was really uncomfortable. I'm sure it looked very great to other people, or even on a rack in the store, but I really didn't like it.

Then came my toddler stage, when I first got to wear pants. That felt pretty good. It changed my life, in fact, because I could run around in the park, or play in the sandbox, or play with the boys. In dresses, I could only sit down and watch all the other kids play. It was kind of like being on a team and having to sit out on the bench, instead of actually being in the game.

When I was around 8 or 9, I finally got to pick out my own clothes. At the time, everyone was wearing ripped jeans, so I decided to rip a pair of my jeans and they looked pretty cool.

One day when my mother and I went to Sears, I wore my ripped jeans and a T-shirt. My mother wore a pair of jeans and sneakers also. To be honest, we looked like homeless bums. My mom bought something, but the salesclerk had forgotten to put one of those "PAID" stickers on it. The security guard stopped us and assumed we were shoplifters. They held us, but my mom refused to show the guard our receipt because he let a well-dressed man walk though the door without making him show his receipt, and he didn't have a sticker either.

In dresses, I could only sit down and watch all the other kids play.

My mom began to fuss and fight, and she complained to the guy who was in charge of the store. After a while of my mom threatening to sue and call lawyers, they let us out. (And my mother never showed the receipt—is that girl power, or what?)

When I was about 10, I began to wear loose-fitting clothes,

such as baggy jeans and big T-shirts. By my sophomore year in high school, I had started to wear men's clothing, such as wide-leg pants and big flannel shirts. At school, I have to wear a uniform, but I wear the boys' version—men's pants and men's oxford shirts. I really like men's clothes, because they give me more room. I think that women's clothes are too confining.

After all of those changes, I've finally found the style that's right for me: baggy, worn-out wide legs, loose shirts, worn-out sneakers and my famous black hat. I think that I like those things because they have been worn through the years, and the more something is worn out, the more comfortable it is.

I don't think that my style fits under any sort of category (unless ya wanna call it Jenish). But I do think that the way I dress says that I am my own person, and that I am a non-conformist. It says that I don't care what people think about me; I am who I am.

Jen was 17 when she wrote this story. She graduated high school and attended college.

Big, Black, and Beautiful

By Anonymous

It took me a long time to convince myself that I am a beautiful girl.

I grew up going to a private school where I was one of only a few black students. At that school, it seemed like only the thin, blond, and big-chested girls were considered appealing.

I am 5'7" and weigh 150 lbs. I am truly a brick house and have been called thick many times. No matter how fit I was, people regularly commented on my size because I wasn't thin and didn't look like a supermodel. Some students would talk about my round butt, thick hair and lips, and shapely figure. "Nobody wants your fat butt," one guy told me.

As a result, I constantly worried about my physical appearance. Whenever I'd get around friends I'd ask, "How does my hair look?" or, "Do I look fat in this outfit?" I was becoming almost annoying.

Because of the comments about my body, I often felt hurt, sad, and angry. Even if my friends and family told me how pretty, smart, or popular I was, the negative comments were the ones that stuck my head.

I'd try to defend myself, but that would only make them bother me even more. They knew the slurs would hurt me, even if what they said was not true.

I felt so bad about myself that when attractive guys looked at me, I'd turn my head and look the other way. I thought I knew what they wanted—white girls, Hispanic girls, or light-skinned black girls with long legs and straight hair. But at the same time, I'd get whistles and catcalls from black and Hispanic guys on the street who said complimentary things about my body. I'd wonder why they bothered. I was the big girl, the fat one.

I thought I knew what guys wanted—white girls, Hispanic girls or light-skinned black girls with long legs and straight hair.

It hurt the most when the boys would call me fat. Most of the guys in my school were white. The ones who weren't liked white girls, or at least the girls who looked like white girls. And since there weren't many black guys in my school, I wanted to please the white guys and look and act the way they wanted me to.

A great thing about my school was that I could date guys of different races and no one would stare or say a thing, because everybody dated each other. But because I dated white guys, my friends outside of school called me a "white girl." They didn't like that I dated out of my race.

And I felt it was not exactly normal, because when my white boyfriends and I would go out to the movies or the mall, we'd get stares. One time an old boyfriend and I were waiting in the train station. A Hispanic guy started to sing "Jungle Fever," a Stevie Wonder song about interracial couples.

My boyfriend and I just looked at each other and started to laugh. But it wasn't funny. It wasn't anyone's business what we did.

Even though I tried to look and act like a white girl with my friends from school, when I hung out with friends outside of school I had to try to act cool, maybe even throw in some slang. But I sounded so stupid that I got picked on even more. I was always called the "white girl" whenever I was around my family or my black friends who didn't go to my school.

"Do you think you have thin lips?" or "Why do you fling your hair like that?" they would ask.

I'd try to ignore their comments, which were about everything from my legs to my hair. But it was hard.

Once, when a friend noticed I was shaving my legs, she looked at me disapprovingly and said, "Black girls don't shave their legs!" I asked her what she meant by that and she said, "Black guys think hairy legs are sexy." I'm not sure that's true, or that it even matters.

My friend also told me that "respectable black women don't show off their stomachs either." Why couldn't she just ask me not to wear that shirt because she didn't like it, instead of making it into a race issue?

I felt as though a day couldn't pass without my friends and family mocking something I did that was totally natural for me. They made a race issue out of my looks, my voice, how I pronounced words, and everything I did.

Their remarks always offended me. What did they mean, talking like a white girl? It was ridiculous! I was proud of the education I got at my school. I didn't know how to talk or act in any other way.

It was horrible. The more I strived to speak like an educated person, the more I was considered a white girl by my own race.

I know it doesn't have to be that way. Last summer I visited

Spelman College, a historically black women's college in Atlanta, Georgia. The alumni there were extremely smart and had perfect diction.

They were also proud of being black and were sure of their culture. They showed me that a black woman can be and sound educated without losing her black identity. But in my old school, and with my friends and family, that didn't seem to be the case.

Finally, I got fed up and decided to transfer to a different school. I was tired of being examined and analyzed by everyone. Shortly after I arrived at my new high school, I began to have a whole new outlook on life. I noticed girls of all different sizes had boyfriends, and fine ones, too. "How did she get him? Look at her size," I would think.

Walking the halls, guys commented on girls' butts—but not the way I was used to. "Look at how round it is, that's so fly," they'd say.

I noticed girls of all different sizes had boyfriends, and fine ones, too

I was really shocked. These guys liked big butts and girls like me? Wow!

I began to forget about my looks and could concentrate on my schoolwork. I knew I had to get my head together, or else. I began to boost up my grades and receive awards. I felt really good about myself because I was able to use education as a way to build myself up. Once my marks rose, I felt great.

At the new school, no one commented on the way I talked, acted or dressed. I was kind of expecting them to say something, but they didn't. I'm not sure if I was losing my "white girl" character, or if they just didn't care.

After a while, I began to compare myself to other black females in my life. Many of my black girl friends love themselves, regardless of what size they are. Where did they get such positive attitudes? My white girl friends from the private school continuously complained about their size and thought they had to be thin to be accepted by men.

It would be great if more white girls had the same positive body image as many black girls. It also would be great if black girls could feel good about showing how educated they are, and would take a lesson from successful black women like the alumni I met at Spelman. Speaking and acting educated doesn't have anything to do with being white or black.

I found out I don't have to look like a white girl or talk like a black girl. It may be best to be right in the middle.

The author was 17 when she wrote this story.

Part 4: Together/Apart

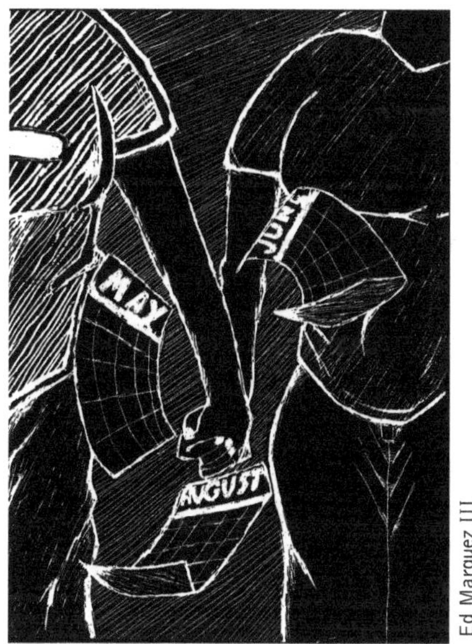

Ed Marquez III

Ready for Mr. Right

By Faleisha Escort

I didn't start developing romantic relationships with guys until my junior year in high school. Before then, I just saw guys as pals that I could always bug out with. When I decided I wanted to start dating, it was mostly because my friends were experimenting with relationships and I wanted to be closer to them and participate in their discussions about their experiences with guys.

Talking to my friends made me curious. They told me things like, "When you're in a relationship, you're supposed to sacrifice for the other person," and, "You got to always keep your man in check." I wanted to find out for myself whether their theories were correct.

I had at least three boyfriends in high school. (I'm in my first year of college now.) I think the main reason I was attracted to these particular guys was the fact that they were easy. Don't get me wrong, I liked them. But the main attraction was that they were easy prey! I already knew that they liked me, so I didn't have to work that hard to get them. They were my relationship guinea pigs.

None of these relationships lasted longer than a month or so, because I wasn't as serious as I thought I was, and neither were the guys. That doesn't mean we didn't exhaust ourselves trying.

But we always ended up playing these roles I wasn't comfortable with. I was "mother," trying to guide and protect my man, while he was "father," the authority figure trying to control me.

I found out my friends were right about having to make sacrifices to be in a relationship—but I was the one doing all the sacrificing. The guys I went out with were always saying things like, "Oh, I want to be with my friends today," or, "I want to see this movie, not that one." I was just expected to sit back and have no opinions or objections.

I was just standing there bored while Derek spent nearly half an hour pumping quarters into the arcade game!

I would go along for a while, doing what they wanted instead of what I wanted. If they asked me to hang out with their friends, I would, even if I didn't really want to. But if I asked them to hang out with my friends, they would just refuse. Of course I got tired of that and ended the relationships. But I still felt disappointed and disenchanted. It seemed like my high school boyfriends just could not get beyond "what I want" or "what I say goes."

The moment I realized I wanted a different kind of relationship came one night last summer when I was out with my (now ex) boyfriend Derek. We were at the movies, killing time, waiting for the show to start. So we went downstairs to the theater's little arcade section to chill. As soon as we got there, Derek headed toward the change machine and began popping quarters in one of the games.

At first I thought, "OK," since we were there and all, but then it got ridiculous. I was just standing there bored while Derek spent nearly half an hour pumping quarter after quarter into the arcade game! He must have gone through at least $5 worth of quarters. And get this: He has the same game at home. I knew right then and there that I was going to break up with him after the movie.

The way he was acting made me feel like I was less important to him than the video games in the arcade. The fact that he was spending all this money (like he was Donald Trump on a spree) combined with his lack of consideration for any of my feelings was the last straw.

Since becoming a free woman again, I've been thinking about what I want from my next relationship and how to go about getting it. For one thing, I have higher standards for myself and I am not going to take just anyone anymore. I'm not going to settle for a guy who is easy to get.

The kind of guy who would immediately spark my interest is, of course, someone who I consider cute, or at least fair, in terms of looks. Hey, looks aren't everything, but they do count! Next comes personality and character. It's important that the guy genuinely likes and cares about the same things I do. (A guy who is cute but boring would immediately be canceled out as relationship material.)

He would be a strong believer in God. He would have had a spiritual upbringing—that's important because that's where he got his basic philosophy about life and his attitudes toward women. He would love and respect his family and get along with them very well. His intelligence level would be equal to mine. And his morals would give him self-respect and respect for the people he cares about.

Lastly, he would not be the type who claims to want a monogamous relationship, but can't seem to stop flirting with other feminine faces. I hate that.

Because I think you need to know all these things about a person before getting serious, I think a successful long-term relationship is most likely to stem from a strong, committed friendship. If you've developed love, trust, and mutual respect as friends and withstood the tests of disagreements, rumors and gossip, etc., then surely you are prepared to handle the not-so-different challenges of a romantic relationship.

I believe that if I develop a meaningful, long-term friendship with a guy I find to be both mentally and physically attractive, then I'd be able to move into a relationship more comfortably than with someone I barely know. Though I was friends with a few of the guys I went out with in high school, they weren't long-term friends. I really didn't know them like I thought I did. Later on I would feel naive. I would say things like, "What the hell did I see in that guy?"

I'm not going to settle for a guy who is easy to get.

Now I will wait, browse around, explore new landscapes (slowly) and develop long, meaningful friendships with guys I am interested in before I decide to move into something more serious. After all, they may be great as pals but nothing more.

After making that transition from a long-term friendship to a romantic relationship, I think I would also feel more secure about the issue of sex (which will surely come up sooner or later). If a guy who has stuck by me emotionally for years asked me to have sex with him, I'd be more comfortable discussing it and more likely to consider it than if a guy I barely knew asked me to have sex with him after only three weeks.

I think the good thing about a long-term relationship with the right guy is the joy and security I would find in sharing my life fully and intimately with another person. I would be able to fall in love completely.

It would also be more of a challenge for me to be with the same person for months and years and still love him enough to not get tired of him. That is the way I love my family and I would really like to experience that with a guy.

A short-term relationship allows you to step in and step out with little or no remorse. A long-term relationship, on the other hand, allows you to get so deeply involved and attached that you can't really help falling in love and truly sharing yourself. One day, I want to be able to say, "Gee, he knows me so well," and, just as important, "Wow, I know him so well."

Do I feel like I'm ready for a long-term relationship? I don't really know, but I am intrigued. I know it would be a challenge to wake up every day and be with the same person for so long and still be committed. But I feel that when I am ready to take that stand, I will be committed all the way.

Faleisha was 18 when she wrote this story. She attended Lehman College, majoring in African-American studies.

Matty DeLuna

From Silent Victim to Self-Confident Sister

By Anonymous

At 14, my confidence and self-worth were at an all-time low. I was very shy. I only spoke when I was spoken to and walked with my head down. In school I tried to act normal because I didn't want to be called weird. I spoke to the quiet, geeky people because I thought the popular, loud people were way out of my league.

That year I had moved from my grandmother's in New Orleans to my mother's in New York, and within six months she was back to using drugs. She used up all the house money, so my sister and I had nothing to eat, and she beat us viciously. I came into foster care feeling hopeless.

Most days after school I went straight home and stayed there. My sister would socialize with the guys around our block and I would stay quiet, feeling self-conscious. I didn't talk to any of the guys because I felt ugly.

But I was desperate for attention, so when I did catch the eye of a 22-year-old named Travis, I soon lost my virginity to him. I believed this man was the only man that would ever want to have sex with me. I felt privileged to have him even waste his time on me.

After we did it, he told all of his friends. I felt hurt and ashamed. It felt good that a man lusted after me, but deep inside I still felt lonely.

Still, I believed that sex would be the way I could get love and affection because I thought my body was all men could see. As far back as elementary school, my encounters with males were very degrading.

The first time I was molested was when I was 4 years old. My brother's friend was in the room with me alone. He was husky and tall with dirt brown skin. I was lying on the bed with panties on and he was standing over me. He asked me, "Can I touch you right there? Promise you won't tell."

"I won't tell," I responded.

I don't know exactly why I let him do it, but afterward I told my grandmother what happened. She told him to leave but a couple of weeks later he was hanging out with my brother again. When I saw him again, I actually felt guilty because I didn't keep my mouth shut.

The next encounter was with another one of my brother's friends. I was about 7 or 8 and we were in the living room. He was sitting on the couch grinning from ear to ear. He told me I was very pretty and he wanted to touch me. To my surprise, he did. My sister was right there. We just looked at one another in shock.

We never spoke about it. As fast as it happened, it left my memory. I made myself forget.

Another time, my sister and I spent the night at my uncle's

house and my cousin was in charge. While my sister and I were in his bedroom watching television, he began tickling us very sexually and inappropriately. We ran out of the room to get away from him. He followed us and pulled his penis out and began waving it back and forth, so again we ran off.

As soon as we got home we told our grandmother. She told my uncle, but she didn't ask how we felt so we didn't really talk about it. After that, my grandmother acted like it never happened and so did my sister. I felt that we had to forget about it, and that no one cared to know how I felt. As I got older, I never thought about these incidents. It became almost like they never happened.

I believed that sex would be the way I could get love and affection, because I thought my body was all men could see.

But when I look back, I think that ever since then I felt that the only way to interest a man was to give up my body. I felt sex was an obligation and not a choice.

For two years after I lost my virginity to Travis, it felt like no guy had an interest in me. During this time, I hung out with friends and kept myself occupied, drowning myself in novels and love songs to deal with the loneliness. Novels were my escape from reality. I imagined I was the girl in those books, getting all the guys' attention. I was beautiful, sexy, in charge, and in love—in my mind. I would daydream about love so much I couldn't concentrate.

As I got older, I had sex with a few other guys and none of those relationships worked out. But it was Davar, a guy I met in Brooklyn, who really hurt me. Davar was the guy I'd dreamed about. He was extremely handsome and rough, with smooth cocoa butter skin and gorgeous brown eyes. He was in a gang and he didn't go to school. I loved that a handsome thug wanted to talk to me.

When I visited Davar for the next few weekends, he made

feel important, pretty and wanted. When Davar didn't call I would get upset. I was in love with him and I wanted him to feel the same.

The last time I visited he asked, "Why are you holding back?"

"I'm not ready to have sex and you should wait until I am," I said shyly. I wanted to have a different kind of experience with him.

But that night I went to Davar's house, and while we were lying in his bed he kept asking me to have sex. I didn't want him to get upset so I said yes. Deep down in my soul I didn't want to but I was afraid he'd leave me if I didn't. It hurt that I couldn't tell him no. I was being submissive and I couldn't help it. I had been putting a man's needs before my own for so long, I found it hard to stand up for myself. Just a couple of days later I realized he'd given me an STD.

After that experience, I started to despise men and myself. I hated myself for what I let men get away with. I felt so worthless and scared of opening up to any guy. I couldn't even be around men. I wouldn't acknowledge any guys on the street and I didn't even want to be near my father, my cousin, my brother—all mankind.

At the time, I wasn't even sure why I was so angry. I really didn't think it was related to the times I was molested because I didn't even think about those experiences. I just felt strongly that the only way to keep myself protected from further hurt was to keep them all out.

For over a year I felt ashamed. I feared that if I told anyone what had happened, I would be viciously criticized. I expected my sister to call me a ho and look down on me. I believed my brothers would be disappointed in me, and I thought my friends would disown me.

But I knew I needed to deal with my fear of men and learn how to deal with relationships and sex. So I thought a lot about why I disregarded my own feelings to please others. Then all the painful moments of my childhood came back to me, and I realized I'd slowly drifted away from myself because I was hurting so much inside.

I wanted so badly to be free of pain and misery that I did whatever I could to change how I felt. I read self-help books and wrote down tips. I talked to my friends about some of my feelings of worthlessness and they gave me good advice.

In a book called *Souls of My Sisters* I found so much inspiration. The black women in the book had been through hell and back and still they were strong. I wanted to emulate them so I started talking to a woman that I thought was strong, a teacher named Ms. Williams. I told her I didn't feel good about myself and she said, "Nobody's going to tell you you're beautiful; you have to believe it yourself and celebrate your beauty."

Every day I have to tell myself I'm worthy until I truly believe it.

When she said that I knew there was no doubt in my mind that I had to begin to love myself. Reading Maya Angelou's poem, "Phenomenal Woman" gave me even more inspiration.

I decided to start speaking my mind, and to begin to face the feelings of rejection I was carrying with me. I decided to stop blaming the guys I'd had sex with for how bad I felt inside, and to work on the hate I feel for myself. I told myself, "Chaquana, you're sassy, courageous, strong, bold and beautiful inside and out."

Since then, my confidence has made a lot of progress.

The most shocking thing I did was tell a guy I didn't like him. I usually don't want to hurt a guy's feelings. But recently I received a phone call from my sister's boyfriend's friend, Jamel, who's in prison. He told me he liked me and he wanted to know if he could take me out when he was released.

"Sure, we could go out, but don't ever think I'll start liking you because I'm not interested," I told him. The old Chaquana would have settled for a guy in jail. The new me spoke up and told him how I felt. That was a huge step for me.

I'm still working on loving myself, and to be honest, it's not that easy. Every day I have to tell myself I'm worthy until I truly believe it. But my plan from now on is to be myself and get my point across. These days I don't get nervous when I pass guys on the street. I used to be scared they wouldn't like me, but my new motto about guys is, "Take me as I am or have nothing at all."

I smile when they talk to me and think to myself, "Yeah, I'm beautiful and I'm sexy but you don't stand a chance." It's funny because they really don't stand a chance. I don't need their attention right now.

The author was 17 when she wrote this story. She graduated from high school and attended Tuskegee University.

Elizabeth Deegan

I Am Religious, Outgoing, Short, African-American, Talented, Honest. . .and Gay

By Anonymous

When I was 12 or 13 years old, I had my first big crush on another girl. I thought Nicolle was incredibly cute and I wanted to date her. I liked Nicolle's sporty style and the way she carried herself.

Plus, she had a really welcoming grin—like the smile of the most popular boy in a book about high school. She carried herself in a "no nonsense" type of way. No one picked on her and she never picked on anyone else. People liked her. She was studious, which was cool, and she also loved basketball. She always played with the boys while I played badminton. I admired her for all the shots she made that the guys did not.

I wasn't good friends with Nicolle. But we'd chat sometimes

or joke around. I cannot pinpoint exactly when I started liking her, but I can always remember glancing at her in class. Or smiling at her when we made eye contact. And if she smiled back at me, which she always did, that was a bonus. It made me feel good to have somebody I liked give me that kind of attention.

Once, though, she invited me to her house, and I kept wishing she would kiss me. I never told her that because I thought she would react weirdly. I thought she might hit me or tell me to get out of her house. Or even worse, she might totally think I was joking. So I never did tell her how I felt. Even though I was not comfortable telling her, I was not surprised about my feelings for her. I thought it was OK to like someone, male or female. It was just another crush to me.

I wanted to let people know that I was proud to be gay, and that I didn't want to hide it.

I knew what gay people were at a young age and I never thought they were weird. At age 8 or 9, my aunt had a gay friend who she told me about. I took it in stride. Occasionally there were people who did not care much for gay people. Generally, though, people around me were more positive than negative. Probably because of that, I was open-minded at a young age. I thought both females and males were beautiful. I thought women were sexy.

Still, I did not immediately come out to myself or to anyone else after I realized my attraction to females. I felt comfortable liking who I liked and I did not feel the need to start calling myself by another name to identify myself. I did not even know that a girl who liked girls always called herself a lesbian or bisexual. I just knew my feelings.

But last year, in October, I finally did come out. I had joined a teen support group for gay, lesbian, transgendered, questioning, bisexual and non-labeling youth. Being in the group made me realize that I was part of a somewhat segregated community, and I wanted to let people know that I was proud to be gay, and that I didn't want to hide it. First I came out as bisexual, but later

I decided that I only wanted to be with other girls.

I was 16 at the time and I was so happy with myself. I told so many of my friends what I knew about myself, and my true friends took it well. I only had a few bad cases. I decided not to tell my friend Dede, for example, because when I brought up gay people in conversation she told me that she did not like lesbians. I was disappointed by her answer and I started drifting away from her.

My 10-year-old sister was the first person I told in my family. "Sarah, do you know what it means to be gay, lesbian, or bisexual?" I asked her.

"Yeah."

"What's a bisexual?"

"I don't know."

"That's a person who likes males and females. They might also have sex with them. OK?"

"Yeah."

Then I said, "Sarah, I'm bisexual. Do you still love me?"

"Of course I do. I don't care what you are," she said.

Then I gave her a hug in the middle of the street. At that moment, it did not matter whether or not the rest of my family accepted me. By opening up to my sister, I felt I paved my way for coming out to the "world."

I told my other siblings (all younger than me, but older than my little sister) a few months later when they kept teasing me and getting on my nerves. I just blew up at them and I told them the truth. They started bugging. My sister threw pencils at me and kept saying she didn't believe me. My brother kept asking me, "Was that girl who slept over your girlfriend? You don't like boys at all?" But after a few days they calmed down. I guess I knew that they accepted me when they asked me real questions like how I knew I liked girls, if I had a girlfriend, and who was the "man" in the relationship.

The questions went on for two or three days. By the time I got a girlfriend in May, it was not an issue.

The hardest person to come out to has been my mom. She hasn't been bad, but she hasn't been totally accepting, either. When I first told her I was bisexual, she told me that she still loved me, and then she gave me a hug and kiss on the cheek. I was pleased about that. But then she said, "Everybody goes through it. It's just a phase." Then she left and I was speechless. I felt betrayed. I knew it was not a phase.

The next day I started going out with my first girlfriend. I met her at a meeting for youth from the gay community. I told my mom immediately so she would not be surprised. She did not take it as well as I expected, but she dealt with it. I invited my mom into my bedroom and said, "Mom, I have something to tell you."

In a wary voice she said, "Don't tell me about your friend. I don't want to know."

"I just want you to know we are girlfriends."

I do not remember what we said after that but I think she asked me something about whether we were having sex. I said no. She left with a smile on her face.

When I told my mom I was bisexual, she said, "It's just a phase."

For a while after that, I didn't feel like I could really talk to my mom. She would ask me whether I was gay or bisexual, or how long it was going to last, and I would get annoyed. Then we had a conversation and she explained how she felt.

Right now she says she does not mind my sexuality. But as a Christian, she wants me to have a close relationship with God, and she says that eventually I'm going to have to decide between my sexuality and God. She says it is either/or.

She still says she supports me no matter what, and she even inquires about my girlfriend. But she also gets annoyed if I bring up her name for no good reason. She let me go to a camp for gay teens, but she does not like my gay friends sleeping over. And I don't think my mom believes that gay people can be in love with each other.

My mom wants me to know that she cares about my happiness, and she lets me know that she loves me daily. But I also know that she thinks I can only be close to God if I decide to be straight. (I was raised very religiously, and actually, that's the one thing I'm still struggling with.)

I haven't been that close to my mom for a while. But since I told her I'm gay, we've grown even more distant. That hurts. And it makes it even more important for me to have other people around who support me. Two of them are Contessa (the sweetest, most beautiful aunt) and Ms. James (a loving second mother to me, and adult confidant).

Being gay is just a part of who I am.

One day, sometime in July or August of this year, I had a really short chat with Ms. James. It went like this. I whispered, "Do you know I have a girlfriend?"

She didn't hear me, so I said, "Do you know that I am gay?" Then I stepped back to look at her face.

She laughed and said, "Yes. It's OK with me, baby. I don't mind. You are still doing good."

Telling my Aunt Contessa was just as nice. When I told her how I felt, she said, "I respect that and I respect you. It's good that you know what you want. When I was about your age, I thought I might have been bisexual. But I figured out I wasn't. It is good that you know and you tell people."

Another thing that has helped me was going to a camp for gay teens for the last week in August. It was so cool. We were near a lake, so I was able to swim and boat. We had campfires, good food, heartfelt group discussions, arts and crafts, games, prizes, a talent show, a dance, a beautiful history lesson about being gay, hacky sack, laughs, cries, scares, powerful rain, blown out lights, and utter fun. We even went swimming at night under a sky full of stars. It was a blast.

This camp was geared to helping gay youth keep a positive attitude about themselves and building small family groups among us. It was a camp for empowering the youth of the gay community. It helped me and a lot of other youth share ourselves more and feel safe and accepted.

I'm gay, but I still feel the way I've always felt most of the time: Content, happy, in love, solid, whole, loved, pressed for time, and loving life. Being gay is just a part of who I am. I am also religious, outgoing, talented, young, pretty, short, African-American, friendly, caring, loving, peaceful, focused, proud, and honest. And I love country music.

I do not feel like I should stand apart from others because of my sexuality. It feels weird if I do. Gay people are no different from the rest of the world and we should not be ridiculed, bashed, fired, looked down upon, feared, or unloved. Being gay is not my lifestyle. It is a part of my life. I love who I am and what I can do. I would be pleased if everyone could accept me, too.

The author was 17 when she wrote this story.
She went on to graduate from high school and attend college, studying psychology and creative writing.

Ed Marquez

Two's a Crowd:
Why I Won't Get Married

By Clariza Sanchez

When I was a little girl, I always dreamed of becoming successful and having a lot of money when I grew up. But I don't remember ever thinking about getting married.

Years later, that still hasn't changed. My mother insists that one day I'll fall in love and get married. I keep telling her that everybody doesn't have to get married to be happy, but she tells me that I will change my mind in a few years. I know I won't.

I've never understood why parents pressure their daughters into marriage. I guess they think that women need men to take care of them, because they don't believe that women will be able to take care of themselves. Some parents also think that in order for their daughters to be happy, they must have a man in their lives. My parents think the whole point of life is to get married and have children.

The only thing I want out of life is money. If I'm financially successful, I won't need anyone to take care of me and I'll be able to do what I want, when I want. That way I'll be able to own the big apartment in lower Manhattan that I've always dreamed of, with a Jacuzzi and a big pool table. I'll also be able to go anywhere I want in the world for vacation.

If I got married, I wouldn't have that kind of freedom. I fear that my whole life would be spent at home taking care of a bunch of people who piss me off every day.

For me, getting married would be like getting attached to a ball and chain for the rest of my life. I mean, why would I want to wake up every single morning and see the same person lying next to me? I know that one day I'd just get really tired of him and the love that used to be there would fly out the window.

The idea of marriage is to have a long-term commitment with one person for the rest of your life. But I don't think I would be able to stay faithful to one person. I would want to go out and flirt with every person I found attractive, so my husband wouldn't be able to trust me at all. And I would expect my husband to be doing the same thing, so I'd have no trust in him. And if there's no trust in a relationship, how long would it be able to last?

My parents think the whole point of life is to get married and have children.

Some people get married because they want a companion, someone to be with all the time. After 14 years of sharing a room with my older sister, I've realized that I don't want to have someone there with me when I wake up and before I go to sleep. Whenever she doesn't get what she wants, my sister stomps around and slams the door. Even if my husband didn't act like that, I don't think a human being exists who wouldn't get on my nerves if we lived together day in and day out. I always find something about a person that makes me unable to stand them after a certain point. That's why I never want to share a room, or an apartment for that matter, with anyone again after I move out of my parents' apartment.

If I had my own space, I could do whatever I wanted without having someone looking over my shoulder all the time, questioning everything that I do. I also wouldn't have to deal with those annoying little things like having to wait my turn to go into the bathroom, or getting interrupted every time I'm on the phone.

Some people assume that if you're not married, you'll be lonely. But if I could get rid of all those problems, I think I would look forward to going home at night—even if there wasn't anyone there to greet me when I opened the door. Just because you live alone doesn't mean you're always going to be alone. At some point, I'm sure I'll have a boyfriend. And although he wouldn't at any time be moving in, he could still be there with me on lonely nights.

There are other reasons why I'm afraid to get married. The main one is that, from what I've seen, men have always had more power in marriage than women. One example of that is how children almost always take their father's last name. It's like they belong to him, like their mother doesn't matter.

If I decide to have children, I want them to take my last name. And I would never take some man's name. Not only would I feel like he owned me, but I would also lose my own identity because Clariza Sanchez would no longer exist.

The second thing that I'm afraid might happen is what's been happening to many women I've seen on television: getting divorced and being left with nothing but the children.

The last thing I'm afraid could happen is that my husband will become tired of me before I become tired of him, and one day, when I decide to come home from work early, I'll find him in our bed with another woman. That, of course, would lead to a divorce that would cost me thousands of dollars that I worked very hard for.

Marriage is supposed to be like a fairy tale. You fall in love with someone, get married, have children, and spend the rest of your lives together. But that's not something I can see myself doing. Other people—like my parents—might think that marriage is why we were put on this earth, but I don't believe that.

I believe that we are here to be happy and everybody has a different thing in their lives that will make them happy. For some it might be getting married and having a family. For others, like me, it's being successful and having a lot of money that counts.

There's no one right way to live. And I don't think I, or anyone else, should feel pressured to get married just because other people think marriage is the key to happiness. I know what I want out of life, and marriage isn't it.

Clariza was in high school when she wrote this story.

Part 5: Hey Baby: You Look Good

What You See Isn't What You Get

By Marcia Persaud

I was going to a party with some friends and I was wearing a very short dress. As I walked down the street, guys were going crazy—making comments, whistling, and blowing their car horns. I ignored them.

Then my friends and I reached a corner where a group of guys was hanging out. They started saying things to me like, "Hey baby, you look good," and "You look sexy."

One of the guys approached me and said, "Hi, sexy." When I did not answer, he said, "How much for a night?"

All the comments were annoying, but that last one really upset me. I was being compared to a hooker just because I was wearing a short skirt? I felt he had crossed a line. He thought he could say anything and get away with it. He should get some respect for girls, I thought.

I stepped up to him and asked him to repeat what he'd said. He did. Then he asked me if I wanted to do something about it. My friends were saying, "Girl, don't take that. Show him what you can do!"

The guy said, "I know you don't have the guts to fight." I couldn't take anymore. I was very nervous but I went up to him and gave him a slap in the face.

My friends, the guy's friends, the people who were just passing by—everyone was stunned. They could not believe what I had done. I could hardly believe it myself. I had never responded to guys before when they harassed me. I would just go my way, partly because I was very shy and partly because I was afraid that if I said anything back, they might want to harass me more.

Everyone who saw what happened started laughing at the guy and making fun of him. All the girls were saying, "Way to go!" to me and some of the guys were saying, "I wish my girlfriend was like you."

I felt awful, fearful, and sorry. I was angry at the guy, but I was also angry at myself.

To cover up his embarrassment, the guy who started with me said he and his friends were coming after me later. But I wasn't scared. I knew they wouldn't be able to find me because I don't live around that area..

Looking back, I am glad that I did not back down. No one in my life had ever said stuff like that to me, so I was determined to make it the first and the last time. That experience made me want to fight for my rights and act proud to be a woman. It even encouraged me to go to the gym and start lifting weights so I would not have to be scared of guys anymore.

Before that, I was always scared to talk back to guys when they said things that I didn't like. Now I know that I don't have to walk by and take nasty treatment that I don't deserve, from people who don't even know me.

But that night, I didn't feel proud or brave. I felt awful, fearful, and sorry at the same time. I never expected someone to say something like that to me, so I was not prepared for it. Afterwards, I was angry at the guy, but I was also angry at myself.

I didn't really think before I acted—what if he'd had a weapon? Something more serious could have happened. And maybe if I hadn't worn that dress, I wouldn't have received those awful comments. "Maybe I shouldn't wear such revealing clothes," I thought.

That's something I think about a lot. I love wearing sexy clothes. I think women should be proud of their bodies and show them off. And I find short skirts more comfortable than long skirts or jeans, especially when it's hot.

The problem is that a lot of people think they can tell something about you by the way you dress. That's not always true. You can wear sexy clothes but not be sexually active.

I don't have a boyfriend or hang out late with my friends. I just like wearing short clothes. Women should feel comfortable wearing whatever we want. There is no need for guys to try to make us feel bad.

Usually when guys say nasty or insulting things on the street, it's because they've tried to get your attention and you've ignored them. They get mad, because their words have gone to waste, so they try to embarrass or shame you. Making a girl feel bad about herself must make them feel important.

And it's not just guys who insult us and try to make us feel bad about ourselves. Other girls do it, too. For example, when a girl goes out with a lot of guys, or if she's slept with a lot guys, she is considered a "slut" by other girls. Sometimes they'll call her that just because she's popular or dresses in a sexy way.

The only reason I can see why one woman would call another woman a slut is jealousy—she probably wishes guys were paying more attention to her. Or maybe she feels unattractive and is trying to build up her own self-esteem by tearing down someone else's. I don't think it should bother other women if a girl dresses sexy or sleeps with a lot of guys, because it is not their business.

It's funny—if a guy has a lot of girlfriends or sleeps around, he is considered a "dude." Other guys encourage him and make him feel proud of what he is doing. But if a girl has a lot of boyfriends or sleeps around, other girls will often insult her or try to make her feel ashamed.

Women should not be ashamed of being attractive or having sex. It's up to you to decide what you want do with your life. It doesn't matter whether you wear short skirts or baggy jeans, whether you're having sex or not.

Someone else will probably have something to say about it, but just ignore them. It's your business. You should feel free to wear what you want and do what you want.

Marcia was 18 when she wrote this story.

Chris Pope

Girls: Dish Out What You Take

By Clariza Sanchez

Hey, girls, have you ever seen a good looking guy with a nice ass and wanted to say, "Hey, cutie. I like the way you look in those jeans?" Have you ever been tempted to grab a guy, or say something fresh about his body? Well, most girls don't act that way, but what's stopping us?

Girls are always complaining about men harassing them, but they never do anything about it. I think it's time for women to treat men the same way they treat us.

I hate the way men harass and abuse women. And I hate the way most women just take it. If all of those idiots who hang out on the corner with absolutely nothing better to do can hiss at every beautiful girl who passes by without thinking twice about it, then why can't those same girls pat a cute guy on the ass when he wears tight jeans?

Instead of complaining about all the men who hiss and grab you when you wear short skirts, do it to them when they wear something tight. If you see a cute guy walking down the street and he's wearing shorts, you could call out something like, "Hey, baby, nice ass!"

Would that be so hard? I mean, it's not like we only like a guy for his personality. I think girls are just as interested in guys' bodies as guys are in girls' bodies.

Many of the girls I know love to talk about men's bodies. They're always saying things like, "Damn, I wish I was the one who got to rub the oil on his body," or "You can tell he has big balls." The only difference between girls and guys is that we only say those things to other girls, while a guy will say what he thinks about a girl's body right to her face when she passes him on the street.

It's time for women to treat men the same way they treat us.

When people ask us what we look for in a guy, girls usually say we want a nice personality or someone who can make us laugh or someone with money. A guy's body is rarely mentioned. But that's only because girls are afraid of what other people (mainly guys) would say if we told the truth.

We don't want people to call us dirty or trashy. We would be too embarrassed, or we just don't have the guts to say what we think of some strange guy's body to his face. But I think we'd be happier and feel more in control if we were the ones making the comments, instead of just being on the receiving end all the time.

I'm sure a few of you are thinking, "I don't like it when guys do that to me—I wouldn't want to do it to them." Well, I think that's why you should. If you don't like guys harassing you, let them find out what it feels like. If they don't like it, too bad. Like the saying goes, "Don't dish it out if you can't take it!"

I think it would be interesting to find out how guys react to this kind of attention. Some might ignore it, while others would probably be flattered. Some might get angry to find themselves on the receiving end of sexual harassment.

If you try this at school you might find yourself getting reported to a teacher or the principal. If that does happen, then you would have to stop (or at least move on to someone else). But, in my opinion, it's worth the risk. I mean, why should we be embarrassed or ashamed to shout out, "Hey baby" when something nice walks by? Guys aren't.

We shouldn't just accept that men get to do whatever they want. Sometimes the best way to get back at a person is by giving him a taste of his own medicine. It's one way of showing that females aren't just going to take every little thing men throw at us. I doubt that this will change the way men react when they see a girl wearing a tight shirt, but at least we'd be speaking our minds.

Clariza was in high school when she wrote this story.

A Very Fine #9 Cutie

By Faleisha Escort

It was 10:15 a.m. when I got on the downtown #9 subway train at 59th Street. I glanced around but there was really nothing to look at (as usual). Then the train pulled into 50th Street and bam! A sexy, chocolate, firm, fine guy got on, looking as hot as Daytona Beach! This guy had body and a cute face to go with it.

I was hypnotized. "Wow!" I said to myself. "I probably won't get a chance to see a hot guy like this for a long time."

As I began to stare openly at Mr. #9 Cutie, I felt a bit daring—like I was crossing a line. This isn't the kind of thing that a "nice girl" is supposed to do, right? I was looking so hard that people began to glance at me, somewhat surprised. But I didn't pay them no mind. After all, these were my eyes to do with what I pleased.

When he first got on the train, I thought that a few quick

looks would satisfy me, but I was wrong. I found myself staring at that man for a good 30 seconds. When he noticed, I felt myself begin to blush, so I glanced away.

I had wanted him to take notice of me, but when he did I grew self-conscious about the way I looked. My hair wasn't done as nicely as I would have liked it to be and I had dressed pretty lazy, just throwing on anything before walking out of the house. I wished that I looked as good as I usually do. But after a minute, my eyes wandered to him again, and this time I took a good long look at his body. Yes! I was looking him up and down with a passion.

He looked like he was between 18 and 21. He was about 6 feet tall and was wearing a long, blue shirt and blue, baggy jeans with a blue baseball cap. He had a nice, firm tone and a nice, firm behind. And his face was cute, too. He had dark brown eyes, firm cheeks, and juicy, luscious lips (the kind you want to dive into).

I saw him catch me staring again so I glanced away. I was beginning to like this silent cat-and-mouse game. It made me feel like I was in control, because I was checking the guy out for a change instead of him checking me. It felt really exciting to be in the dominant position with a guy I found attractive. It felt good to express my sexuality in that way.

Girls often feel like they have to repress those kinds of feelings. I think that's bad because when the time does come when you do want to attract a guy and let him know how you feel, you may not know how. These days, when girls see another female coming on to a guy they like, they become bitter and resentful because they're not comfortable enough with their own sexuality to make a move.

I don't want to find myself in a situation like that. Checking out a guy like Mr. #9 Cutie is a way of practicing for when the real thing comes along.

The train passed 34th Street and I noticed that the object of my attentions seemed rather indifferent to the fact that I was checking him out. I could tell by the look he gave me that he was quite used to having girls stare at him. He did not smile or anything, he just knew he was fine. This disappointed me, especially since I was pretty sure that if I had looked better that day, he would have taken more of an interest.

Although this was the first time I'd tried this on the train, it was not the first time I had checked a guy out so aggressively. I had done that once before at my school.

It was my junior year in high school and he was in my earth science class. I hadn't really noticed Jonathan until one day when he bent over to pick up a piece of paper, giving me quite a lovely view of his rear end.

I sat at the back of the classroom with a clear view of Jonathan's table. Every time he went to bend down, there was my view. There were times when I really couldn't avoid seeing his "bouncy buns" and after a while, I didn't want to! I was a female pervert and I knew it.

I had never felt so conscious of admiring a guy's body before. This was a new experience for me and I was enjoying it. It made me feel kind of bold. I know that some people think girls are dirty when they stare at boys in a sexual manner, even though they think it's natural for a guy to stare at a girl like that. I wanted to defy that double standard.

And I didn't stop with looking. The attraction was so strong that I decided to let Jonathan know what I was feeling about him (or at least his body).

One day I decided to write him a devilish little note saying a little something-something. So I wrote, "I think you have a nice ass," on a piece of paper, folded it up, and kept it for the right moment.

Since the water fountain was right behind Jonathan's desk, I pretended to get a drink. Then I walked by his desk and tossed the note discreetly down by the side of his notebook, making sure he saw it.

As he opened the note, I was anxious. I thought he would

look at me as if I was crazy or something (which I wouldn't have minded since I was taking a walk on the wild side). Instead, he just looked back at me and smiled as if to say "Really?" or "Wow, that's what you think?!"

I could tell he was flattered. And I felt relieved and pretty macho; I felt like I was a sexually aggressive female who knew what she was after and wasn't afraid to pursue it. I was pretty proud of myself and feeling good. And since my little note got such a positive reaction, I just had to take things a little further...

To make a long story short, I made the mistake of chasing Jonathan down and pursuing him mercilessly. I would hang around him as much as possible and find out everything I could about him. One time we had to write a poem for our creative writing class describing our special characteristics. Since Jonathan wasn't providing me with enough information, I snuck into his class folder and read his poem. I was pretty obsessed.

I wanted to prove to myself that I could be sexually aggressive and get what I wanted, just like a guy.

I don't think I was hoping for a serious relationship, but I did want to prove to myself that I could be sexually aggressive and get what I wanted, just like a guy.

One time I called Jonathan up and he asked me, "Do you consider me as just a sex object?" and I said, "Yes."

I was being honest. But he seemed somewhat offended by my frank response. And he refused my advances, which made me mad. I just could not accept the fact that he did not like me the way I liked him, especially after his initial positive reaction to my note.

Back to the man on the #9 train. When my stop—28th Street—arrived, I began to get off and to my surprise, so did he. But I got off ahead of him so I didn't see where he went—and I didn't want to.

Although I feel good when I boldly check out cute guys, I still feel uncomfortable about chasing them too hard after what happened with Jonathan. Besides, I got my mental photograph of the #9 cutie for future reference and there will be more cuties to see!

Both these situations started with my giving the guy the same kind of look, but they ended very differently. With the guy on the train, I was basically flirting—even if he wasn't flirting back. With Jonathan, what I did turned into a kind of sexual harassment because I did not want to take "no" for an answer. I looked at Jonathan as a "boy toy" and not as a real person with real feelings. I forgot how much I hate it when guys I am not attracted to do that to me.

But I will continue to look. And, since I'm comfortable making the first move, too, I will continue to do that as well. Turning the tables on guys that way makes me feel in control and a bit bold. And that's a good way to feel.

Faleisha was 18 when she wrote this story. She attended Lehman College, majoring in African-American studies.

FICTION SPECIAL

Matter of Trust

Darcy Wills clenched her hands so hard that her fingernails dug into her palms. Hakeem Randall was walking to the front of the classroom to give his English report on Macbeth. He was a good student, but when he got nervous, he stuttered. Darcy dreaded this moment. She knew that if he began to stutter, the class would show no mercy. Just thinking about how embarrassed he would be made her cringe.

"Oh, Tarah," Darcy whispered to her friend, "I feel so *bad* for him!"

Tarah Carson turned a stern eye on Darcy, "Girl, he gotta fight this battle himself by doin' just what he's doin', facin' it."

Darcy had been dating Hakeem for just a few weeks, but at times it seemed that she had known him forever. He was a tall, handsome boy with a lot going for him—he was a good student, a great singer and guitar player, and a really nice person.

"My report on *Macbeth,*" Hakeem began, "is about how

This is the first chapter from *Matter of Trust*, by Anne Schraff, a novel about teens facing difficult situations like the ones you read about in this book. *Matter of Trust* is one of many books in the Bluford Series™ by Townsend Press.

g-g-guilt p-pplayed an important p-p-part in the story." Darcy's worst fears were coming true. She had never heard him stutter so badly. A soft ripple of laughter began in the back row and spread around the room.

Mr. Keenan, the teacher, glared at the students. "Let's try to remember this is tenth grade English, not second grade recess!" he growled. It did not help much. Hakeem struggled on with his report, stuttering often. Stifled giggles erupted throughout the room, gurgling like an underg round spring. Roylin Bailey was making a big show of covering his mouth with both hands while he rocked back and forth.

"T-t-tomorrow, and t-t-tomorrow, and t-t-tomorrow," Hakeem stammered, "creeps in this p-p-petty p-p-pace from day to day—"

"Is 't-t-tomorrow' the same thing as 'tomorrow,' Mr. Keenan?" Roylin asked cruelly. "'Cause I want to know, sir."

Tarah's boyfriend, Cooper Hodden, just shook his head while other kids laughed. Cringing, Tarah shrank down in her seat. This was as hard for Hakeem's friends to watch as it was for Hakeem to endure, Darcy thought. Then, finally, mercifully, Hakeem's report was over, and he fled to his desk like a soldier racing across a battlefield and diving into a safe ditch.

Darcy reached over and covered Hakeem's hand with hers, whispering, "It was a good report."

Hakeem pulled his hand away, anger flaring in his usually warm eyes. "I made a fool of myself," he said bitterly.

Through the rest of the class, Hakeem sat staring at his desk and fiddling so violently with his pencil that he broke it in two. Darcy knew he was reliving the humiliation of the report. He told her once that he would replay his stuttering spells over and over in his mind. His speech therapist said there was nothing really wrong with him—it was something he would eventually overcome. But not today.

When the bell rang, Darcy hurried after Hakeem. "Hakeem,

it wasn't that bad, really it wasn't!" she assured him.

Hakeem slammed his fist into his open palm and shook his head. "It was stupid! I'm stupid! If I wasn't stupid, I could talk right!"

"Hey man," Cooper said, standing in front of the snack machines, "don't sweat it. We all feel stupid sometimes. Once, I gave an oral presentation, and people were laughing but I didn't know why. Then the teacher whispered to me that my fly was unzipped."

"Yeah, and he was wearin' bright red boxer shorts that day," Tarah chimed in, smirking.

Hakeem jammed change into the soda-machine slot. He yanked out the can and walked away without saying anything. When Darcy tried to follow him, Tarah grabbed her wrist. "Girl," Tarah scolded, "give it a rest. We all got our lumps and bumps, and nobody gets outta this world without bein' banged up. It's not the end of the world that Hakeem messed up on a report. Let him work it out his own self."

Darcy reluctantly let Hakeem walk down the corridor alone. She felt so bad for him. Right now he was hating himself, and she understood that. Darcy had hated herself all through middle school and her first year at Bluford High because boys just seemed to ignore her. Every other girl in her class seemed prettier, more popular, and Darcy's shyness hurt something like Hakeem's stutter must have.

Darcy walked slowly towards the library to work on a science report. Her father had offered to take her to the Palomar Observatory for the report. The observatory would have made a great topic, but Darcy turned him down. Her father had been away from the family for five years, and now he was trying to rebuild his relationship with them. But Darcy felt awkward and strange with him.

Now she felt estranged from Hakeem too. He was hurting so much, and he would not let her try to help.

As Darcy reached the library, she noticed a flyer posted on the door:

Talent show auditions.

February 20, Noon.

Singers, musicians, dancers, artists.

The depressing thoughts of a moment ago were suddenly forgotten. Darcy's heart raced with excitement over what this could mean for Hakeem.

Everyone knew he was a great guitar player and a wonderful singer. When he sang, he never stuttered. Darcy could not wait till school was over so she could track him down. This show was just what he needed to boost his spirits.

After school, Darcy found Hakeem sitting under the pepper tree behind the Bluford parking lot. His guitar was resting on his lap. She sat beside him on the grass and said, "Did you hear about the auditions for the talent show? You'd be just great for that, Hakeem. You'd blow 'em away!"

"Yeah, watch the stuttering idiot perform. Maybe I could do a ventriloquist act so the kids'll think the dummy is the one who stutters!" Hakeem said bitterly.

"But you don't stutter when you sing," Darcy pointed out.

"I guess," he said, rolling a red berry between his fingers and watching the papery skin pop off, leaving a little brown seed. "Why don't *you* audition, Darcy? You have a nice singing voice. And you don't stutter."

"Oh, I'm no singer," Darcy blushed. "Sure you are," Hakeem insisted. "I've heard you. And you told me you used to sing in a church choir."

"But that's because Mom made me."

"Well, you should really enter this contest. It might give you that spark to start singing again."

"I will if you will," Darcy said impulsively, though the very thought of performing before the student body made her shudder.

Hakeem finally smiled. "Okay. Deal. Maybe we'll both make such fools of ourselves we'll have to run away to a desert island and hide."

Darcy glanced at her watch. A neighbor, Ms. Harris, was sitting with Darcy's grandmother, but Darcy still had to be home soon. "Gotta go now," she said. "Grandma will be needing me."

"How is she?" Hakeem asked.

Darcy shrugged. Grandma hadn't been well since her stroke a year and a half ago. "She's about the same. Some days, she's, you know, almost like normal for a few hours, and then she's back to thinking she's a little girl in her mom's house. I think she always knows me. I mean, she calls me 'Angelcake,' and she's always got a smile for me."

"Your parents getting any closer?" Hakeem asked.

"Dad goes down to the hospital where Mom works, and sometimes they talk in the cafeteria. I don't know if Mom would ever let him come back or even if he wants to. He's just trying to make up for what happened, you know, for running out on us."

"You want your parents together again, Darcy?"

"I don't know. Dad gets along good with Jamee. Even when we were little, she was always closer to him than I was. Maybe it's because she's two years younger than me, and Dad was always ready to baby her. I think right now she's ready to forgive him, but I can't say I am ready to do that. Maybe I should, but it's hard," Darcy admitted.

Hakeem gave Darcy a quick hug. "Like Tarah is always saying, 'We gotta make the best of what we got 'cause there ain't nothin' else to do!'"

They both laughed, and Hakeem picked up his guitar. He strummed a melody and began to sing in his rich, deep voice:

Will you hear me if I cry,
Above the thunder of anger,
Over blasts of fear and hate, When help comes not at all,
Or when it comes too late?

When streets explode with fire,
And hearts grow dead with grief,
When all the sounds are sad,
And there's no more relief?
Will you hear me if I cry?
Will you come before I die?

"Did you just write that?" Darcy asked.

"A couple of weeks ago. I was visiting my cousins, and we were talking about Russell Walker, that guy who went down in a drive-by shooting last year. I sort of wrote it for him."

"Yeah, I heard about him," Darcy said. "He was an honor student and an athlete, wasn't he?"

Hakeem nodded somberly.

"That was a crying shame," she added. "I hope they catch the guys who did it and put them behind bars for good."

Darcy was heading home when she ran into Brisana Meeks. Until just a few weeks ago, they had been best friends. When Darcy started hanging out with Tarah, Cooper and their friends, Brisana cut off the friendship. Since then, Darcy had made small efforts to repair their relationship. "Hey, Brisana," Darcy said, "how's it going?"

"Terrific," Brisana said with a sharp edge to her voice. Brisana had once told Darcy that she and Darcy were the bright, sophisticated kids at Bluford High. They were the "tens." It was their duty to avoid the low-class, stupid kids like Tarah and Cooper, who were zeroes.

"Want to go to the mall on Saturday, Brisana?" Darcy asked.

"With *you*?" Brisana scoffed, placing her hands on her hips. "No thanks," she added, leaving Darcy speechless.

As Darcy walked on, Roylin Bailey pulled up alongside her in a teal-blue Honda. "Hey Darcy, want a lift?" he shouted.

"No, thanks," Darcy said.

"Come on, Darcy," Roylin persisted. "Why are you wastin' your time with that stuttering fool? Sistah, I'm here to tell you, he ain't the one."

"Roylin, leave me alone. I don't remember asking for your opinion on my social life," Darcy snapped.

"Relax, girl. I'm just tryin' to help you out. You know, pass on the male perspective. And from where I'm sittin' you could do a lot better than Ha-ke-keke-keem," he said, snickering.

Out of the corner of her eye, Darcy saw Cooper Hodden's beat-up truck roll up behind the Honda. Tarah, sitting beside Cooper, yelled, "Cooper, baby, you know your brakes ain't so good. Don't go smashin' that Honda now!"

"I can't stop!" Cooper howled, hitting the horn and blasting Roylin's Honda out of his path. Both Cooper and Tarah doubled over laughing as Roylin sped away.

"You guys are outta your minds!" Darcy said, also laughing. "Thanks, I owe you." Leaning in the truck window, she confided, "Hey, guess what. I told Hakeem I'd sign up for the talent show that's coming up, just to make him try out. Problem is, I'm terrified of getting up in front of all those people. And then there's the issue of my voice."

"What's wrong with your voice?" Cooper asked. "You talkin' okay right now."

"No, my *singing* voice. It doesn't exactly make people jump to their feet with applause. Fall to their knees begging me to stop, maybe, but not jump to their feet," Darcy said.

"Girl, don't even worry about it," Tarah advised. "Just play the music real loud, smile real pretty, and nobody'll notice how you sing."

"Thanks, I'll keep that in mind," Darcy replied sarcastically.

D a rcy climbed into the cramped front seat of the pickup truck for a ride home just as Hakeem sped by on a shiny silver motorbike. Hakeem did not seem to notice Darcy, but she saw him—with Brisana Meeks sitting behind him with her arms around his waist.

"That's weird," Darcy said. "I haven't even seen his new bike, and there she is riding on it."

"He prob'ly just givin' her a lift," Tarah said.

"Don't know about that," Cooper chimed in. "That girl's *fine*."

Tarah nudged Cooper in the ribs with her elbow, and he howled. But the damage was done. It was done the minute Darcy saw Brisana riding on Hakeem's motorbike.

"Brisana always used to make fun of Hakeem because he stuttered," Darcy said.

"Stuck-up girl like her, she prob'ly just going after him to mess with your head," Tarah replied.

Or maybe, Darcy thought, *I like Hakeem a lot more than he likes me*. A cold chill pressed down on Darcy's chest like a heavy blanket of ice.

Teens:
How to Get More Out of This Book

Self-help: The teens who wrote the stories in this book did so because they hope that telling their stories will help readers who are facing similar challenges. They want you to know that you are not alone, and that taking specific steps can help you manage or overcome very difficult situations. They've done their best to be clear about the actions that worked for them so you can see if they'll work for you.

Writing: You can also use the book to improve your writing skills. Each teen in this book wrote 5-10 drafts of his or her story before it was published. If you read the stories closely you'll see that the teens work to include a beginning, a middle, and an end, and good scenes, description, dialogue, and anecdotes (little stories). To improve your writing, take a look at how these writers construct their stories. Try some of their techniques in your own writing.

Reading: Finally, you'll notice that we include the first chapter from a Bluford Series novel in this book, alongside the true stories by teens. We hope you'll like it enough to continue reading. The more you read, the more you'll strengthen your reading skills. Teens at Youth Communication like the Bluford novels because they explore themes similar to those in their own stories. Your school may already have the Bluford books. If not, you can order them online for only $1.

Resources on the Web

We will occasionally post Think About It questions on our website, www.youthcomm.org, to accompany stories in this and other Youth Communication books. We try out the questions with teens and post the ones they like best. Many teens report that writing answers to those questions in a journal is very helpful.

How to Use This Book in Staff Training

Staff say that reading these stories gives them greater insight into what teens are thinking and feeling, and new strategies for working with them. You can help the staff you work with by using these stories as case studies.

Select one story to read in the group, and ask staff to identify and discuss the main issue facing the teen. There may be disagreement about this, based on the background and experience of staff. That is fine. One point of the exercise is that teens have complex lives and needs. Adults can probably be more effective if they don't focus too narrowly and can see several dimensions of their clients.

Ask staff: What issues or feelings does the story provoke in them? What kind of help do they think the teen wants? What interventions are likely to be most promising? Least effective? Why? How would you build trust with the teen writer? How have other adults failed the teen, and how might that affect his or her willingness to accept help? What other resources would be helpful to this teen, such as peer support, a mentor, counseling, family therapy, etc.

Resources on the Web

From time to time we will post Think About It questions on our website, www.youthcomm.org, to accompany stories in this and other Youth Communication books. We try out the questions with teens and post the ones that they find most effective. We'll also post lesson for some of the stories. Adults can use the questions and lessons in workshops.

Discussion Guide

Teachers and Staff:
How to Use This Book in Groups

When working with teens individually or in groups, using these stories can help young people face difficult issues in a way that feels safe to them. That's because talking about the issues in the stories usually feels safer to teens than talking about those same issues in their own lives. Addressing issues through the stories allows for some personal distance; they hit close to home, but not too close. Talking about them opens up a safe place for reflection. As teens gain confidence talking about the issues in the stories, they usually become more comfortable talking about those issues in their own lives.

Below are general questions that can help you lead discussions about the stories, which help teens and staff reflect on the issues in their own work and lives. In most cases you can read a story and conduct a discussion in one 45-minute session. Teens are usually happy to read the stories aloud, with each teen reading a paragraph or two. (Allow teens to pass if they don't want to read.) It takes 10-15 minutes to read a story straight through. However, it is often more effective to let workshop participants make comments and discuss the story as you go along. The workshop leader may even want to annotate her copy of the story beforehand with key questions.

If teens read the story ahead of time or silently, it's good to break the ice with a few questions that get everyone on the same page: Who is the main character? How old is she? What happened to her? How did she respond? Etc. Another good starting question is: "What stood out for you in the story?" Go around the room and let each person briefly mention one thing.

Then move on to open-ended questions, which encourage participants to think more deeply about what the writers were feeling, the choices they faced, and they actions they took. There are no right or wrong answers to the open-ended questions. Open-ended questions encourage participants to think about how the themes, emotions and choices in the stories relate to their own lives. Here are some examples of open-ended questions that we have found to be effective. You can use variations of these questions with almost any story in this book.

—What main problem or challenge did the writer face?

—What choices did the teen have in trying to deal with the problem?

—Which way of dealing with the problem was most effective for the teen? Why?

—What strengths, skills, or resources did the teen use to address the challenge?

—If you were in the writer's shoes, what would you have done?

—What could adults have done better to help this young person?

—What have you learned by reading this story that you didn't know before?

—What, if anything, will you do differently after reading this story?

—What surprised you in this story?

—Do you have a different view of this issue, or see a different way of dealing with it, after reading this story? Why or why not?

Credits

The stories in this book originally appeared in the following Youth Communication publications:

"Womanhood Can Wait," by Nicole Hawkins, *New Youth Connections,* September/October 1998

"Trying Femininity on for Size," by Debbie Seraphin, *New Youth Connections,* March 1999

"Thinking for Myself," by Anonymous, *New Youth Connections,* March 2006

"Mama Said..." by Clariza Sanchez, *New Youth Connections,* September/October 1998

"Our Parents' Rules: Fair or Square?" by Miranda Chung, *New Youth Connections,* September/October 1998

"House Arrest," by Anonymous, *New Youth Connections,* September/October, 1998

"University of Kitchen?" by Orruba Almansouri, *New Youth Connections,* March 2009

"Fashion Un-Conscious," by Nadishia Forbes, *New Youth Connections,* March 1999

"The Identity Experiment," by Lily Mai, *New Youth Connections,* March 2006

"Suits Me," by Jen Butler, *New Youth Connections,* March 1999

"Big, Black and Beautiful," by Anonymous, *New Youth Connections,* December 1997

"Ready for Mr. Right," by Faleisha Escort, *New Youth Connections,* March 1999

"From Silent Victim to Self-Confident Sister," by Anonymous, *Represent,* January/February 2007

"I Am Religious, Outgoing, Short, African-American, Talented, Honest...and Gay," by Anonymous, *New Youth Connections,* December 1998

"Two's a Crowd: Why I Won't Get Married," by Clariza Sanchez, *New Youth Connections,* November 1998

"Don't Judge Me By My Short Skirt," by Marcia Persaud, *New Youth Connections,* November 1998

"Girls: Dish Out What You Take," by Clariza Sanchez, *New Youth Connections,* September/October 1998

"A Very Fine #9 Cutie, " by Faleisha Escort, *New Youth Connections,* September/October 1998

About Youth Communication

Youth Communication, founded in 1980, is a nonprofit youth development program located in New York City whose mission is to teach writing, journalism, and leadership skills. The teenagers we train become writers for our websites and books and for two print magazines, *New Youth Connections,* a general-interest youth magazine, and *Represent,* a magazine by and for young people in foster care.

Each year, up to 100 young people participate in Youth Communication's school-year and summer journalism workshops where they work under the direction of full-time professional editors. Most are African American, Latino, or Asian, and many are recent immigrants. The opportunity to reach their peers with accurate portrayals of their lives and important self-help information motivates the young writers to create powerful stories.

Our goal is to run a strong youth development program in which teens produce high quality stories that inform and inspire their peers. Doing so requires us to be sensitive to the complicated lives and emotions of the teen participants while also providing an intellectually rigorous experience. We achieve that goal in the writing/teaching/editing relationship, which is the core of our program.

Our teaching and editorial process begins with discussions

between adult editors and the teen staff. In those meetings, the teens and the editors work together to identify the most important issues in the teens' lives and to figure out how those issues can be turned into stories that will resonate with teen readers.

Once story topics are chosen, students begin the process of crafting their stories. For a personal story, that means revisiting events in one's past to understand their significance for the future. For a commentary, it means developing a logical and persuasive point of view. For a reported story, it means gathering information through research and interviews. Students look inward and outward as they try to make sense of their experiences and the world around them and find the points of intersection between personal and social concerns. That process can take a few weeks or a few months. Stories frequently go through ten or more drafts as students work under the guidance of their editors, the way any professional writer does.

Many of the students who walk through our doors have uneven skills, as a result of poor education, living under extremely stressful conditions, or coming from homes where English is a second language. Yet, to complete their stories, students must successfully perform a wide range of activities, including writing and rewriting, reading, discussion, reflection, research, interviewing, and typing. They must work as members of a team and they must accept individual responsibility. They learn to provide constructive criticism, and to accept it. They engage in explorations of truthfulness, fairness, and accuracy. They meet deadlines. They must develop the audacity to believe that they have something important to say and the humility to recognize that saying it well is not a process of instant gratification. Rather, it usually requires a long, hard struggle through many discussions and much rewriting.

It would be impossible to teach these skills and dispositions as separate, disconnected topics, like grammar, ethics, or assertiveness. However, we find that students make rapid progress when they are learning skills in the context of an inquiry that is personally significant to them and that will benefit their peers.

When teens publish their stories—in *New Youth Connections* and *Represent*, on the web, and in other publications—they reach tens of thousands of teen and adult readers. Teachers, counselors, social workers, and other adults circulate the stories to young people in their classes and out-of-school youth programs. Adults tell us that teens in their programs—including many who are ordinarily resistant to reading—clamor for the stories. Teen readers report that the stories give them information they can't get anywhere else, and inspire them to reflect on their lives and open lines of communication with adults.

Writers usually participate in our program for one semester, though some stay much longer. Years later, many of them report that working here was a turning point in their lives—that it helped them acquire the confidence and skills that they needed for success in college and careers. Scores of our graduates have overcome tremendous obstacles to become journalists, writers, and novelists. They include National Book Award finalist Edwidge Danticat, novelist Ernesto Quinonez, writer Veronica Chambers and *New York Times* reporter Rachel Swarns. Hundreds more are working in law, business, and other careers. Many are teachers, principals, and youth workers, and several have started nonprofit youth programs themselves and work as mentors—helping another generation of young people develop their skills and find their voices.

Youth Communication is a nonprofit educational corporation. Contributions are gratefully accepted and are tax deductible to the fullest extent of the law.

To make a contribution, or for information about our publications and programs, including our catalog of over 100 books and curricula for hard-to-reach teens, see www.youthcomm.org

About The Editors

Andrea Estepa edited *New Youth Connections,* Youth Communication's magazine by and for New York City Teens, from 1991 to 1997. Prior to that, she was a reporter for *The Hartford Courant* and the *Los Angeles Times*. In 1997 she was awarded a Revson Fellowship by Columbia University. Estepa has a master's degree from the Graduate School of Journalism at Columbia and a bachelor's degree from Brown University. She is currently teaching history at the college level and finishing her doctorate in history of women and gender from Rutgers University.

Keith Hefner co-founded Youth Communication in 1980 and has directed it ever since. He is the recipient of the Luther P. Jackson Education Award from the New York Association of Black Journalists and a MacArthur Fellowship. He was also a Revson Fellow at Columbia University.

Laura Longhine is the editorial director at Youth Communication. She edited *Represent,* Youth Communication's magazine by and for youth in foster care, for three years, and has written for a variety of publications. She has a BA in English from Tufts University and an MS in Journalism from Columbia University.

More Helpful Books From Youth Comunication

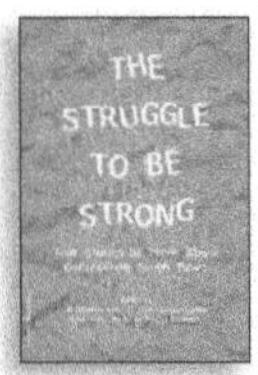

The Struggle to Be Strong: True Stories by Teens About Overcoming Tough Times. Foreword by Veronica Chambers. Help young people identify and build on their own strengths with 30 personal stories about resiliency. (Free Spirit)

Starting With "I": Personal Stories by Teenagers. "Who am I and who do I want to become?" Thirty-five stories examine this question through the lens of race, ethnicity, gender, sexuality, family, and more. Increase this book's value with the free Teacher's Guide, available from youthcomm.org. (Youth Communication)

Real Stories, Real Teens. Inspire teens to read and recognize their strengths with this collection of 26 true stories by teens. The young writers describe how they overcame significant challenges and stayed true to themselves. Also includes the first chapters from three novels in the Bluford Series. (Youth Communication)

The Courage to Be Yourself: True Stories by Teens About Cliques, Conflicts, and Overcoming Peer Pressure. In 26 first-person stories, teens write about their lives with searing honesty. These stories will inspire young readers to reflect on their own lives, work through their problems, and help them discover who they really are. (Free Spirit)

Out With It: Gay and Straight Teens Write About Homosexuality. Break stereotypes and provide support with this unflinching look at gay life from a teen's perspective. With a focus on urban youth, this book also includes several heterosexual teens' transformative experiences with gay peers. (Youth Communication)

Things Get Hectic: Teens Write About the Violence That Surrounds Them. Violence is commonplace in many teens' lives, be it bullying, gangs, dating, or family relationships. Hear the experiences of victims, perpetrators, and witnesses through more than 50 real-world stories. (Youth Communication)

From Dropout to Achiever: Teens Write About School. Help teens overcome the challenges of graduating, which may involve overcoming family problems, bouncing back from a bad semester, or even dropping out for a time. These teens show how they achieve academic success. (Youth Communication)

My Secret Addiction: Teens Write About Cutting. These true accounts of cutting, or self-mutilation, offer a window into the personal and family situations that lead to this secret habit, and show how teens can get the help they need. (Youth Communication)

Sticks and Stones: Teens Write About Bullying. Shed light on bullying, as told from the perspectives of the bully, the victim, and the witness. These stories show why bullying occurs, the harm it causes, and how it might be prevented. (Youth Communication)

Boys to Men: Teens Write About Becoming a Man. The young men in this book write about confronting the challenges of growing up. Their honesty and courage make them role models for teens who are bombarded with contradictory messages about what it means to be a man. (Youth Communication)

Through Thick and Thin: Teens Write About Obesity, Eating Disorders, and Self Image. Help teens who struggle with obesity, eating disorders, and body weight issues. These stories show the pressures teens face when they are confronted by unrealistic standards for physical appearance, and how emotions can affect the way we eat. (Youth Communication)

To order these and other books, go to:
www.youthcomm.org
or call 212-279-0708 x115

www.ingramcontent.com/pod-product-compliance
Lightning Source LLC
LaVergne TN
LVHW010102110826
845155LV00028B/449

* 9 7 8 1 9 3 3 9 3 9 9 2 6 *